"*Cape, Spandex, Briefcase* illuminates lessons for leaders through character, plot and dialogue. David Kahn gets to the heart of organizational dysfunction and offers his insights into how good leaders can and should prevail. The book is spot on for new leaders and those who want to up their skill set. Kahn clearly understands how relationships are the basis of a successful leader."
— JOHN BALDONI, Top 50 Inc.com Leadership Expert and author of 13 books including *MOXIE: The Secret to Bold and Gutsy Leadership*

"*Cape, Spandex, Briefcase* helps you become the superhero leader you want to be while recognizing the very human challenges that you'll face along the way."
— MARC EFFRON, Author, *One Page Talent Management*

"In his first full-length book, Dr. Kahn reaches past common tropes to write a wholly new style of business book. *Cape, Spandex, and Briefcase* is a modern management fable for the forward-thinking MBA and comic fan alike."
— JOSH LEVINE, Co-Founder, CULTURE LABx

"This wonderfully written book contains deep business and life lessons from the great superhero stories. Reading it, you'll have unexpected fun and get to the bottom of some of the most important issues for true excellence in anything you do."
— TOM MORRIS, Author of such books as *If Aristotle Ran General Motors, Superheroes and Philosophy,* and *The Oasis Within*

"Superheroes are simultaneously alluring and untouchable. They are human, like us, but something more. In *Cape, Spandex, Briefcase*, David Kahn reminds us that *we* created these characters. They are made in our image, and our capacity for leadership resides not in otherworldly powers, but in understanding and utilizing that which is uniquely human inside us."
— SEAN R. MCMAHON, Professor, Elon University; Founder, Knowtro, Inc.

"*Cape, Spandex, Briefcase: Leadership Lessons from Superheroes* is a lighthearted and fun read on some very serious leadership topics. I thoroughly enjoyed the characters and storyline but was especially impressed with the superb lessons on how to be more successful and effective leader. A great book to add to your leadership collection."
— JOHN SPENCE, *Top 100 Business Thought Leader in America*

"What happens when an author writes an entertaining story and adds in the key principles of leadership? Kahn's new book *Cape, Spandex, Briefcase: Leadership Lessons from Superheroes* is what happens. This compelling story helps the reader think differently about one's self and others. In the process, Kahn achieves what every great author dreams of, namely, writing a book that drives personal and professional change."
— ORRIN WOODWARD, Guinness World Record Holder, Inc Magazine Top 20 Leader and NY Times Bestselling Author

This is a big day for you...gonna go out in the world and make a difference. Whatever you do, remember that. You're going to make a difference. A lot of times it won't be huge, it won't be visible, even. But it will matter, just the same. Don't do it for praise or money, that's what I want to tell you. Do it because it needs to be done. Do it to make your world better...just a little at a time.

— Police Commissioner James Gordon, Gotham State University graduation commencement

from *Gotham Central: In the Line of Duty*

Cape, Spandex, Briefcase

Leadership Lessons from Superheroes

Cape, Spandex, Briefcase

Leadership Lessons from Superheroes

David Kahn, Ph.D.

STAREWELL

 STAREWELL PUBLICATIONS

Copyright © David Kahn, 2015

All rights reserved

13 12 11 10 9 8 7 6 5 4

First published in 2015 by Starewell

LIBRARY OF CONGRESS CATALOGING IN PUBLICATION DATA

Kahn, David

    Cape, spandex, briefcase : leadership lessons from superheroes / David Kahn.
    p. cm.

ISBN 0692530703

1. Leadership.   2. Success in business. .   I. Title

Printed in the United States of America

To my family who make me feel like a superhero
and my friends who remind me that my powers are limited.

Contents

1

The Hero

At the public relations firm POW! PR, Inc. Ben was renowned as an up-and-coming star. Once hired, Ben gained a reputation for his work ethic and passion. Ben was on the fast track, advancing to an account executive position and rising through the ranks on his way towards his ultimate goal of making partner.

Within a few short years, Ben was promoted to executive director, the youngest in POW! PR's history. His dreams were coming true... or so he thought. This was his first time managing his own department, and it was not nearly as fulfilling as he had expected.

The big-picture initiatives Ben was once shielded from mixed with the minutiae of the workday, plus juggling the personalities of those on his team was taking its toll. Ben used to half-jokingly introduce himself as the future CEO of POW! PR. Now he was unsure why he had wanted to be a leader at all. Was it naivety or outright stupidity?

Either way, this was not the time to get lost in self-analysis. Today Ben was pitching a new campaign to the whale of all accounts. This one client would make up for every failed proposal in the last five months and would mark an end to his horrendous dry spell. This was a defining moment in Ben's career.

"Take another deep breath," Ben whispered to himself as he gathered the strength to get out of his car. "Today has got to be better than yesterday."

Ben knew this was unlikely, but what choice did he have? The client meeting was beginning soon and the longer he procrastinated, the harder it would be to open the door. After mustering the energy to get out of the car, enter the building, and walk into his department, Ben realized he was right to be anxious.

Mary Jane, one of Ben's best account representatives, was frazzled as she peppered Ben with questions about the presentation to the client. "Who's going to be in this meeting?" she asked.

"Didn't we determine this last week?" Ben said with not-so-veiled frustration. "We are expecting four representatives from the client."

"That was last week," Mary Jane responded. "Last I heard we have eight, including their CEO."

"Their CEO is going to be here? Why wasn't I told about this sooner?"

T. Thomas Tylerson was the CEO of Gulag Corp. His vision had turned Gulag into a premier sports drink brand. Tylerson had a reputation for being generous and kind, but he was also known to be blunt, almost to the point of cruelty. He was a busy man and did not like his time to be wasted.

"I don't know why you didn't know this, Ben. I told your assistant twice," Mary Jane said.

Ben held back his aggravation. "No problem," he said, "we have two hours to adjust the presentation for Tylerson."

"Two hours? We have fifteen minutes," said Mary Jane.

Not again. This was the third time this month that Betty, Ben's assistant, had mis-scheduled an appointment. He'd have to deal with it later.

As the panic set in, Ben heard his creative team shouting at each other from the other end of the office. The topic was unclear, but Cliff, Larry, and Rita were prone to loud debates. "What gives you the authority to change my photographs?" Larry shouted. "You shouldn't even have access to my drafts!"

"We have the same level of access," Rita responded, "and without my graphics, your images are useless."

"Would you two please shut up," Cliff barked. "I'm actually trying to get some work done."

"Seriously?" Larry yelled as Ben rushed to his meeting, pretending not to hear this exchange.

After his less-than-graceful sprint down the hall, Ben struggled to restrain his panting as he greeted his guests. The next twenty minutes were a blur. Ben had rehearsed incessantly for this presentation. His team may be falling apart, but Ben always shined when pitching to clients.

Just as Ben felt like he was getting into his groove, Tylerson interrupted. "I'm not going to mince words. This pitch is not good. You've already quoted me inaccurate numbers, stale visuals, and a campaign eerily familiar to what we did a few years ago."

To Ben's surprise, Tylerson then stood up and walked out of the conference room.

Ben wasn't sure if he was nauseous from the abrupt conclusion of the meeting or the impromptu cardio workout he'd gone through to get there. Either way, his sickness was justified.

After the meeting dissipated and everyone had scattered, James, the vice president of Ben's division, told Ben to wait for him in his office. As if the day could get any worse.

Ben had never been called to a VP's office. It's amazing how much this felt like being sent to the principal – the fear of being in trouble, the flurry of irrational punishments.

"What am I so scared of?" Ben asked himself. "James is a standup guy. He might yell, but I can take it. Wait, will he yell?" In all his time at POW! PR Ben had never heard James raise his voice to anyone.

James was well-liked throughout the company, although some questioned what he did all day. Ben never put stock in the gossip, but he'd heard the rumors that James landed a big account years ago and had been coasting ever since.

If Ben had any complaints about James, it was that James always appeared to be so calm. "You can't be that composed if you're actually working," thought Ben, who lived by the philosophy that the faster you walk, the more people will know you are busy. "Maybe a VP's life is just easier."

Ben sat in James' office for five long minutes before James sauntered through the doors with, "What the hell, Ben?"

Before Ben could answer, James followed up with, "Tylerson just told me how disappointed he was with the pitch."

"Yeah, he made that pretty clear," Ben said as he slouched further into his chair. "Let me just say the client was--"

"This is bigger than one client. Help me understand how a department that was leading the company last year can be in such a slump? I don't get it."

"That's true, but--"

"And, I heard Mary Jane wants to transfer to another team. Did you know she was unhappy?"

"No, but--"

"She's your top performer, Ben. How do you not know? It's not like she has any ability to hide her emotions."

"James, you can't take Mary Jane. She's all I have." Ben took a breath to collect himself. Mary Jane was the superstar of the team. She had been with POW! PR since long before Ben had joined and she'd earned a reputation as the go-to account representative. When the manager position opened up, Mary Jane was a vocal supporter of Ben's, stating he'd be perfect.

"See if you can convince her to stay. If you can't, I'm approving the transfer. Fair?"

"Yes, but--"

"But Mary Jane is not your only issue, Ben. Your whole team is falling apart. Not to mention the missed deadlines and sloppy mistakes." James stopped and leaned back in his chair. "Ben, I want you to be successful, I really do. But you won't tell me what you need." He was sincere and Ben knew it. "I've been offering help since you started in this position, haven't I? We need a new strategy."

Ben winced. He knew what was about to happen; he'd been bracing for it since his first week as director. "I'm sorry I put you in this position, James. Just get it over with," Ben said while trying to avoid eye contact. He was starting to sweat again and this time it had nothing to do with running through the halls.

"Do you think I'm going to fire you? Don't be so dramatic. If I fired every director who had a bad quarter...."

"I've had two."

"And that's why we need a new strategy."

Ben exhaled but did not feel any sense of relief. "I'm not oblivious. I know this department is floundering. And I know it's my fault."

"Then my first question is whether you still want to lead this team. If you don't, I will find something else for you. I like you and I know you're talented. So, do you want this?"

"I do," said Ben, but he wasn't certain.

"Good, because we have a second chance at the Gulag account. I'm not sure if anyone told you, Ben, but Tylerson is familiar with a few of your team's past campaigns. That's why he specially requested you."

"I wasn't aware."

"Well, lucky for you he's seen your team's potential. He'll be back next week. Think you can be there on time?"

"Funny, James. You mentioned a new strategy?"

"It's something I should have urged you to do before you took this promotion," James said. "I'm sending you to this leadership guy I know. His methods are unconventional, but he knows his stuff."

"Like an executive coach?"

"Of sorts. He developed a secret formula of leadership a while back, but you'll need to keep an open mind. Like I said, he's unconventional."

"Give it to me straight. Are you sending me to some type of new-age, sweat-lodge, primal-screaming, walk-on-hot-coals leadership development trendy retreat?"

"Would you go if I did?"

"Yes."

"Well, I appreciate you trusting me, but I wouldn't do that to you. My assistant will give you the details. He's expecting you at noon."

As Ben walked out of James' office, he felt better knowing there was hope. James still believed in him, even if Ben didn't quite believe in himself. He was so caught up in the last few hours that he unknowingly walked past James' assistant towards the elevator. Thankfully, she got his attention before he was confronted by another emergency.

"Does James send a lot of people to this guy?" Ben asked as he fished for more information.

"Rarely," she responded with a smirk. "His methods are not for everyone, but it's effective if you're willing to learn. Here's the address. It's not too far from here."

"Thanks, any idea how long it'll last? I have a ton to get done this afternoon."

"The first meeting is usually pretty short."

"The first? How many are there?" Ben said with concern. He needed all the time he could get to prepare for next week's pitch.

"That depends," she said with amusement. "Some people don't get a second meeting. It's best to consider this an interview. If he sees your potential and you're willing to take his pledge, the training will continue."

"Pledge?" Ben said with surprise. He had presumed this mystery trainer would give him a few pointers to get him going.

"He'll explain when you get there," she said.

What kind of pledge? And what if this guy didn't feel Ben was worthy? On most days this impending rejection would have thrown Ben into a nervous mess. Fortunately, the morning had beaten him into a state of emotional numbness.

"Good luck," Ben heard as he drifted towards the corridor.

2

The Pledge

A few hours later, Ben pulled out of the parking lot heading to the mysterious address. He was still nervous but it was time to focus his energy on preparing for the "interview."

What could this guy possibly ask? The possibilities were endless. "Was there going to be a test?" Ben thought. "What if I don't pass?" Ben was always good at interviewing, but this was different. His past interviews were to get a job, not to keep it.

Before Ben could get too wound up, he arrived at a strip mall. There was nothing out of the ordinary about it; in fact, he was a frequent patron of the coffee shop on the far left side. Being in such a fragile state, Ben didn't think he could handle the caffeine boost so he went directly to his appointment.

When Ben saw his destination, he let out a chuckle. He had passed this store a hundred times. How could he have missed it?

In a less inhabited corner of the shopping plaza was an obnoxiously decorated storefront. Covering the windows were posters and cardboard cutouts with a wide variety of cartoon characters. There was not an inch of open space. The first layer of prints was worn by sunlight, with each consecutive coating behind it appearing brighter.

Ben parked and walked up to the store. He wanted to organize his thoughts before opening the vibrant, paraphernalia-plastered door; however, the visual was overwhelming. There was so much to see that Ben could not focus on any one thing. The only exceptions were the red neon word "Comics" and the blinking "Open" sign.

When Ben opened the door to the comic book store, it chimed to announce his entrance. Actually, it wasn't a chime; it sounded more like a laser gun from a science fiction movie. What an appropriate way to enter into this foreign world.

The outside window displays were nothing compared to the colorful characters lining the walls. Spaceships and planetary shapes were hanging from the ceiling. Action figure toys were exhibited like fine works of art in an upscale museum. And there were books everywhere – comic books, hardback books, and trade magazines, each with imposing, muscle-bound individuals adorning the covers.

The bins seemed to be organized in a manner Ben could not quite grasp. Some said "sale" or "new arrivals," but most had headings and sub-headings with unfamiliar names. The smell was not quite musty, though it was distinct with the aroma of paper, ink, a hint of popcorn.

Ben wasn't sure how long he'd been standing in the doorway taking in the view before he heard someone say, "Welcome to Blaze Comics."

Ben followed the voice to the back of the store. Sitting on a stool near the checkout was a guy in jeans, a faded t-shirt, and an untucked flannel. On some people, this attire might have been sloppy, but this guy wore it with a composure that seemed to match his personality.

He was older than Ben had expected, with a display of sureness Ben found to be intimidating. It wasn't a fearful intimidation; it was more about being in the presence of someone who was completely comfortable with who he was.

As Ben walked towards him, the man stood and extended his hand.

"You must be Ben. Nice to meet you. The name's Perry but please call me Chief; all my friends do. I appreciate you taking the time to meet on such short notice."

Ben felt immediately at ease. He couldn't describe why; it just felt natural. He was considering the reason Chief was thanking him, but this thought was interrupted when the glass door swung open with a voice shouting, "Yes, Chief! Emphatically, without a doubt, the answer is yes! To be a superhero, you've gotta have powers."

"Olsen, Ben. Ben, Olsen. Pardon me for a second. We've been debating this for weeks and I think he's finally ready for his retort."

"Superheroes, by definition, have extraordinary abilities not held by normal people. That's in the dictionary, Chief. Powers are what define them as superheroes. Superman's ability to leap tall buildings in a single bound and move faster than a speeding bullet is what makes him a superhero.

Without those and every other power he possesses, he's just a guy wearing blue tights," Olsen said with a passion that made Ben uncomfortable.

"Can we agree Superman is a superhero?" Chief asked.

"Of course," Olsen hastily responded.

"Good, just wanted to make sure we're on common ground," Chief said with a nonchalance that seemed to make Olsen even more irate than he already was. "Since his inception, Superman has consistently held two universal principles. The first is that he puts the needs of others before himself. Second, he does not give up, regardless of the obstacle in his way."

Olsen stared intently at Chief, waiting for him to put this into context.

"Powers do not make someone a superhero any more than wearing a costume does. If you don't believe me, Superman said this in Season 10, Episode 18 of *Smallville* – a 'hero is made in the moment by the choices he makes and the reasons he makes them.' Superman does *not* say a hero must be more powerful than a locomotive."

Chief casually leaned back, perfectly in time with Olsen deflating like a balloon with a slow leak. Defeated, Olsen slumped towards the door. In an overly friendly tone, Chief said, "See you tomorrow tonight?"

"Yeah yeah," Olsen mumbled as the laser gun door chimed.

Chief's gaze returned to Ben. "Sorry about that," he said. "We have some avid fans. If I had to guess, I'd say some enjoy arguing about comics more than reading 'em. Everything okay? You've got a look on your face."

"Why, because I just witnessed two grown men carrying on about superheroes?" Ben thought, but he refrained from saying anything. He didn't have to; Chief picked up on his judgmental expression.

"This must seem pretty unusual to you, Ben. When James made this appointment, I'm sure you weren't expecting to be standing in a comic book store. Am I right?"

Ben was embarrassed as he nodded in agreement.

"You don't have to answer that. You look like a serious guy who discusses serious topics. So let's get down to business, shall we? Start by telling me about your last conversation with the CEO of GE."

"Excuse me?" Ben said bewildered.

"Clearly you are too mature and well-educated to engage in a conversation about cartoons. I can only assume you've acquired your knowledge through the time you've spent with the CEO of one of America's most renowned companies. It may have been a different Fortune 100 leader; I don't know what social circles you associate with. Either way, tell me what you two discussed."

Ben was still confused. Was Chief making fun of him or did James greatly exaggerate Ben's status to Chief?

"Judging by the look on your face, I'll take it you've never hung out with any multimillionaire tycoons. That is shocking. How'd you learn anything about business?" Chief asked.

"I read books...."

"You read books? Wonderful," Chief joked. "So, to clarify, you didn't get any actual face time with the people you admire? Typical case of our public school system dropping the ball."

"But I've learned a lot from their biographies and interviews," Ben said defensively.

"Of course you have," Chief responded with a tonal shift into absolute sincerity. "My point is that you and most of the world have the same access to GE's CEO as we do to Superman. Their behaviors, activities, and traits are legendary. Yet, the closest most people can expect to get with either the internationally known CEO or the superhero is by watching them on TV or reading about their latest adventures. Think about it. The likelihood of grabbing a beer with Jack Welch is about the same as having breakfast with Spider-Man. It does not make either of them less influential or inspirational. They both have a message to share, a set of values that can shape how we make decisions, and a vision that can help us lead a fulfilling life. Just this morning, I read about your CEO in the business section battling with his shareholders while I watched Captain America battle some aliens. Who's to say which was more real?"

"I can tell you firsthand that my CEO's battle, as you call it, is very real. What's also real is that his battle is a direct result of my division falling short of the objectives laid out for us," Ben said.

"Actually, he shortchanged the European market and overvalued the potential revenue of his pet projects that had no hope of making the significant impact he sold to shareholders at last quarter's meeting," Chief countered.

Once again, Ben could not mask his emotions. Who was this guy? One minute he's arguing about a cartoon, the next he's giving a lecture on international business practices.

"Don't look so surprised, young Jedi. Just because I'm in a place specializing in fantasy worlds, doesn't mean I live in one. You've gotta open your mind to the possibility that valuable information is not always accompanied by a suit and tie. Knowledge can be gained in unlikely places from seemingly unlikely people."

"I'm starting to see that," Ben thought.

"Just to finish my point, there are many great people who can serve as role models," Chief continued. "However we don't need personal contact to learn from them. They don't even have to be real. We've been learning from myths since the beginning of mankind. The Greek gods, Knights of the Round Table, and Robin Hood and his Merry Men were all fabled heroes of their time. They personified a moral code in a way that a bullet-pointed list of rules could never have accomplished. Does this make sense, Ben?"

Ben's head was spinning. This was making sense. Had he underestimated Chief or had the day taken its toll on his ability to think clearly? Either way, Ben was intrigued. He wanted to ask more questions about Chief's analysis of the European market but decided this could wait.

There was one last nagging question. "Why do you want to help me?" Ben asked.

"Because you have the potential to be a leader."

"Aren't I a leader already?" Ben wasn't being defensive. Even if he didn't feel much like a leader, he had been promoted to a leadership role.

"This is a good place to start. Were you listening to my debate with Olsen?"

"Sure, he said Superman was a superhero because of his powers and you said it was about his actions."

"Very good. So I'll ask you, what makes someone a superhero?"

"I would have gone with superpowers, but that's clearly not correct. The ability to do things ordinary people cannot do?" Ben said apprehensively.

"I like that answer. It's incorrect, but I do like it. What's lacking is accessibility."

"Accessibility?"

"Yeah, it sounds unattainable. You're saying that us ordinary folks 'cannot' perform superhero feats, whereas I say we 'choose' not to do them."

"People choose not to fly?"

"You're getting caught up in the superpowers. Remember, it's about the hero's actions."

Ben thought about these actions. It wasn't easy to distinguish them from superpowers.

"I can tell you're contemplating this, Ben. And I appreciate you taking it seriously. I don't want to spoil this moment, but we are having an intellectual discussion about superheroes. Anyway, I'm going to jump to the answer. Do you want to know what makes a superhero?"

Ben nodded.

"My secret formula for making a superhero is coincidentally the same as that of a great leader. Although I will say it's not much of a formula, unless having one ingredient is worthy of the phrase. And I have never tried to keep it a secret. You ready?"

Chief straightened up in his stool.

"Courage."

Ben let it sink in before he asked, "And what else?"

"That's it," Chief responded. "The secret formula of leadership is courage."

"So that's all I need? If I'm brave, everything else will follow?"

"In some respects. Having courage is the foundation for being a great leader. If our training continues, we can discuss its application. For now, I just want to make sure we understand each other."

"Why is courage the prerequisite? I know plenty of bosses who I wouldn't describe as courageous."

"That's because most people in leadership positions are not good leaders. They are self-serving and take the easy way out. You know what takes courage? Sacrificing yourself while defending Earth against a violent, villainous monster."

"Excuse me?"

"Picture it. You're Earth's only defense against a giant alien monster. You have no backup, and you're almost out of ammunition. You have two choices. The first is to run away. It's rational and no one would think less of you. Heck, no one would even know you were ever there. The other choice is to use the last of your powers. This will destroy the monster and save Earth, but it will also kill you. What do you do?"

Chief took a dramatic breath before he continued. "Abin Sur chose to save the world."

"Abin Sur?"

"Have you ever heard of the Green Lantern Corps? No? Abin was considered to be one of the greatest members of this elite interstellar police force. You may be familiar with the Green Lanterns from their power ring. This ring has been referred to as 'the most potent weapon in the universe' and is controlled through willpower."

"So are you saying I need more jewelry or that I should stop being scared?"

"No and no. In the book *Kilowog #1*, one of the boot camp instructors for the Green Lantern Corps said, 'You have the ability to overcome great fear. The operative word is *ability*.' What he's saying is courage is not the absence of fear; it's the ability to persevere through it. Willpower is how a Green Lantern does this."

"Quite frankly, I'm concerned," said Ben. "I am not a particularly brave person."

"What makes you say that?"

"I've never been much of a risk taker. I studied hard, got good grades, graduated from college and have had a steady job ever since. I follow the rules and do what I am supposed to do. Nothing exciting or daring," said Ben.

"Why are you here?"

"Here?"

"Yes, why are you standing in this comic book store talking to me?"

"Because I want to be a better leader."

"Well look who's showing courage."

"Huh?" said Ben.

"When you walked in, you were timid and apprehensive. Yet, we are still talking. That's courage. It's about overcoming doubts and insecurities so you can try new things, challenge core beliefs, and maybe take a chance. You ever hear Albert Einstein's definition of insanity? You know, doing the same thing over and over again and expecting different results? That's also the definition of bad leadership. It takes a courageous leader to say, 'We've been on the wrong path for too long; it's time to create a new one.' By standing here talking to me, you are showing a willingness to try a new leadership path. Seems pretty brave to me."

"I never thought of it that way."

"I like you, Ben. I think I can help. Are you interested in learning what I call the Five Superpowers of Leaders?"

"Does this mean I passed the interview? "Ben said with excitement.

Chief smiled. "The only thing left is the Pledge."

The Pledge? Ben had totally forgotten about the Pledge. "How much will this cost?" he asked.

"Ha! You are funny," said Chief. "This isn't PBS. There is no pledge drive. My Pledge is more like an oath, a promise."

This felt worse than money, but Ben instinctively put his right hand over his heart.

"What is wrong with you, man?" Chief said between chuckles. "Would you relax? Put your hand down. My Pledge is very simple, but it is non-negotiable. I'll say it, and if you agree, we'll continue. If you don't, we'll shake hands and consider this a fine conversation. No pressure. Deal?"

"Deal."

"Here it goes. 'In brightest day, in darkest night, no evil will escape my sight. Let those who worship evil's might, beware my power! Green Lantern's light.'"

Ben did not know how to respond. Before he could, Chief snickered. "Just kidding. That's the Green Lantern's oath. Mine is much simpler. All I ask is that you pledge to practice whatever you learn."

"Seems reasonable," said Ben.

"Other people have tripped up on this, so let me clarify before you agree. I don't mean you need to think about the lessons. You must actually do it before the next lesson. That's the only way to fully understand the Five Superpowers.

Practice and experience. It's the best way to change behaviors."

"Will there be a test?" Ben inquired. He was concerned about whether James would know he was making progress.

"This isn't school and I'm not grading you. You'll know if it's working by how others treat you. If you don't follow my Pledge, then you are doing yourself a disservice. I can only provide the opportunity to learn; I cannot make you change."

Ben nodded.

"So we're in agreement?" Chief asked as he extended his hand.

"We are," said Ben.

"Fantastic. I've drafted a schedule for the week. If you're free, let's start tonight. Oh, and here are some reading materials to help you prepare. I'm excited about this. You have the courage and drive; we're just going to give you the other skills to back it up. You're like a young Ralph Hanley."

"Who?"

"You know, *The Greatest American Hero*? Classic show from the early '80's. Oh geez, don't you ever watch TV? Check it out sometime. Anyway, it's about this guy who receives a superhero costume. Whenever he puts it on, he has superpowers. The problem is that he lost the instruction guide. The whole television series is about him learning to use and control his powers. This is you. You were given the suit and all the powers accompanying it, but no one has taught you how to use them."

"Until now?"

"Until now."

3

The Power of Accountability

A few short hours later, Ben arrived back at Blaze Comics for his appointment. He did not know what awaited him this evening except that he was going to hear the First Leadership Power.

Ben was still skeptical about whether the secret formula of courage was the answer to all his problems, but his doubt was overshadowed by his curiosity about Chief. "This guy works in a comic book store and yet he carries himself like the CEO of a Fortune 500 company," Ben thought. "And where did he pull that information about POW! PR? I'm on the inside and I never put those dots together."

When Ben opened the door to the comic book store, Chief hastily walked up and shook his hand.

"Good to see you, Ben. Glad you could make it."

"Thanks, I--"

"No time. Come check this out."

What started as a handshake quickly became Chief pulling Ben to a large table in the center of the store. Standing around this table were seven guys. Six of them did not speak or move. They just stared in awe at something in the middle of the table. The seventh guy was smiling as if he alone knew the secret of the universe.

Ben followed their gaze to an old-looking comic book, then stood there for a minute waiting for something to happen before he whispered to Chief, "What am I looking at?"

"A piece of history," Chief whispered back. "They'll be ogling for a bit longer. Let's move over there to talk."

As Chief and Ben walked towards a rack of comic books on the far right wall, Chief said, "Incredible, wasn't it?"

"The comic book? I guess," Ben cautiously replied. "Looked pretty old. I bet it's worth a few bucks."

"If you consider $400,000 a lot of money, then you're right."

"Seriously? Amazing."

"That's one way of looking at it. Many people see collecting comic books as an investment. While I respect their business acumen, I tend to be more interested in what's in the book. What you just saw was *Amazing Fantasy #15*, the 1960 debut of one of the most established superheroes in the world. Stop me if this sounds familiar. On the streets of New York, a young man watches helplessly as his Uncle is killed in a carjacking gone awry. He soon realizes that he could have prevented his Uncle's murder if he had just stopped the fleeing criminal earlier in the day. The bandit's prior escape was not the result of this young man's fear or inability to subdue the crook. After all, he is virtually unstoppable with his super-strength and spider-like reflexes. He could have effortlessly restrained the thief. Instead he saw the offense being committed, stepped aside as the soon-to-be-murderer ran past him, and denied accountability, stating, 'I missed the part where this is my problem.'"

"We're talking about Spider-Man," Ben confirmed. While not an avid comic book reader, Spider-Man's story was known to just about anyone with even a casual acquaintance with pop culture.

"Not yet. Right now we're talking about Peter Parker," Chief said.

"But Peter Parker *is* Spider-Man."

"Peter Parker *will be* Spider-Man. Before the slaying of his Uncle, Peter's a super-powered profiteer who purposefully did not intervene in the bad guy's getaway because he was more concerned with his own sense of self-importance and entitlement."

It seemed like a subtle distinction, but Ben could see Chief's point.

"Consumed with guilt over the role his indifference played in his beloved Uncle's untimely death, Peter vows to follow his Uncle's mantra – 'With great power there must also come great responsibility.' From this point forward, Peter pledges to use his special abilities for altruistic purposes. He will protect the unprotected and never again act as an apathetic bystander to wrongdoings. This is a pivotal moment for Peter. This is when he became a superhero."

"I just want to make sure I understand you. Peter did not turn into Spider-Man when the radioactive spider bit him?"

"Correct," Chief said with an affirming nod. "He had all the abilities but had not yet accepted the responsibility of Spider-Man the superhero. So let me ask you – the leadership bug bit you when you were promoted. You now have all the power, but have you fully accepted your responsibility as leader?"

Ben wasn't sure how to respond. He had taken the job, but that didn't sound like the right answer.

"I'm not sure," Ben said.

"This leads me to think you haven't." Before this could sink in, Chief jumped to another topic. "Did you read those books I gave you?"

"I did. They were, um, interesting," Ben said with hesitation.

"I'm going to ignore your lack of enthusiasm," Chief said with a smirk. "Did you notice any trends?"

"Yeah, they were all about how someone became a superhero."

"In comic book land, we call those origin stories, and they all have something in common. Superheroes have a moment of clarity when they affirm their new role, thereby making the leap from civilian to protagonist. In many of the recent superhero movies, there's a climactic scene when the hero declares in a bold, almost defiant tone, 'I am Green Lantern' or Daredevil, Kick-Ass, whatever. You've seen it a hundred times. This acknowledgment marks the instant they recognize and accept their new obligations."

"I vividly remember Christian Bale saying, 'I am Batman' in the *Dark Knight* movie," Ben said, proud that he was able to relate on Chief's level.

"And how did he say it? Was he bragging?"

"Not really," Ben said. "It was more like he was announcing it."

"We are going to make a comic book fan out of you yet, Ben. You are correct. Bale was stating, 'I own this new responsibility. I am making the conscious decision to put myself in harm's way to protect others.' Leaders need to make a similar proclamation. So repeat after me, 'I am a leader.'"

"I am a leader," Ben said awkwardly.

"Weak attempt. I know this feels uncomfortable, and I recognize saying it does not make it a reality, but you need to keep reciting this mantra until you believe it. Leaders, especially new ones, must express their purpose and avow they are a leader. While it may seem like a small gesture, this act is significant in the pursuit of taking the leadership mantle."

"I don't know, it sounds kind of hokey."

"Are you familiar with Claude Steele's research on self-affirmation?"

"Was Claude a steelworker who had an accident in the warehouse that turned him into a half man, half robot?" Ben said with a smile.

"Funny. No, he's an internationally acclaimed researcher who first proposed the theory of self-affirmation. You familiar? No? He found that the act of affirming one's stance better enables people to deal with threatening events and information without compromising core values."

Ben gave Chief a blank stare.

"Put simply, the more you say it to yourself, the more you'll believe it. The more you believe it, the more you'll live it," Chief explained. "Peter Parker realized he could no longer sit back and watch injustices occur. He always had it in him; unfortunately, it took a tragedy to bring it out. For you, I will guess that your mounting defeats are your tragedy. You've probably been striving towards this promotion since you were hired. Am I right?"

Ben nodded.

"And, before this promotion, you were successful in every job you'd ever had."

Ben nodded again.

"Now, you feel helpless as all your hard work is carjacked and slain right before your eyes. Strong analogy, but I want you to see that you are Peter Parker, with all the talent, skill and potential of a superhero. Now's the time to proclaim you're the leader. The only other option is to admit defeat, and you don't seem the type."

"I want this," Ben said. He could feel something stirring in the pit of his stomach. There was an energy he hadn't felt in a while.

"Sorry, did you say something?"

"I want this," Ben said louder.

"Why?" Chief asked in a challenging tone.

"I want to prove I can do this. Not because I'm supposed to, but because I am the best person to do it. My entire career has led to this job and if I don't give it everything I've got, I will always regret it."

"I just got goose bumps," Chief said. "Seriously, that was beautiful. You just took the first step towards owning your leadership. Now the real work begins."

Chief excused himself for a few minutes to rejoin the group circled around the infamous comic book. Ben browsed through a rack of used books until he heard a ruckus. By the time he walked over, things had settled down. A minute later, money was being exchanged, and the man with the grin was walking out the store.

"What just happened?" Ben asked Chief. "Did you buy his book?"

"It's a bit out of my price range. Nah, I'm renting it."

"You can do that?"

"Why not? I'm paying him a small fee to display it in my store for a month or two. If someone is interested in purchasing it, I'll get a cut. If not, no biggie. Just having it in the store will bring in more foot traffic from curious bystanders."

"If it's such a good deal, what caused the argument?"

"Primarily, the book owner had unrealistic expectations about its worth, which set off a bidding war. He had a fighting chance, but he lacked the confidence to win over the crowd."

"He lacked the confidence?"

"Sure. He could recite all the facts and figures to illustrate the market value of the book, which were spot on. His problem was in the delivery. There was no certainty behind his words. He thought that by merely owning the book, he would be considered the undisputed authority. He did not count on six obsessive fans who eat, drink, and sleep this stuff. They pushed and he crumbled."

"What'd you do?" Ben asked.

"I let the 'experts' have their fun and then I stopped it. In the end, we compromised. Our arrangement will give me time to do some proper research, and he'll have an opportunity to attract some interested buyers. He might have gotten higher rent from me without the crowd's reaction, but the final sale of the book will make it worthwhile. Everyone's a winner."

"I don't see where confidence ties in," Ben said.

"Let's talk about the series arc in *Batman: Hush*," Chief said switching gears. "In it, Superman is unwillingly committing crimes while under mind control. It's up to Batman to free his ally from the hypnotic power. Part of Batman's plan involves fighting Superman as a means of baiting him into saving Lois Lane, hoping this will break the spell."

"Sounds dangerous," Ben said. "Superman would destroy Batman in a fight."

"I've got a store full of people who would love to debate you on this. For now, let's focus on the anecdote. In preparation for battle, Batman relies on Catwoman, who is understandably apprehensive about brawling with the almighty Superman. Catwoman says, 'You've studied Superman, haven't you?'

'He's the best at what he does,' Batman replies.

'That's open to debate,' she says with skepticism.

Batman then reassures her with, 'I said he's the best at what he does. Not at what I do.'

Batman says this without being cocky or mean. As far as he's concerned, he is stating a fact – 'Superman is the best at what he does; I am the best at what I do.'"

"How is this Batman story different from the Spider-Man story?" Ben asked.

"How do you mean?"

"Weren't they both owning their role as a superhero?"

"Very astute. It's related, but not the same. When we were discussing Spider-Man, Peter Parker had an internal monologue to build his confidence with his new role as a superhero. The Batman story demonstrates how he projects this confidence to others."

Chief looked away for a second to wave to a customer as she walked out the door.

"Where was I? Oh yeah, Batman is a character known for his confidence. He's displayed his competencies and skills on many occasions and has no lack of self-assuredness. As Batman said, he's the best at what he does. In this instance, Batman is certain his plan is thoroughly conceived and he has no reluctance to carry it out. So let's say you're Catwoman and I ask you to provoke one of the single most powerful individuals on the planet. If I were to say, 'I'm pretty sure it'll work. Let's see what happens,' how likely are you to stick around?"

"Not very."

"Right, but because Batman displays poise and certitude, Catwoman is more secure in her assignment and is willing to be part of this dangerous mission."

Ben immediately thought about his team. If they aren't following him, maybe it's because he hasn't shown them that he has the confidence to be in charge. How many times in the last few months had he avoided making difficult decisions or ignored issues a 'real' leader would have addressed? The more Ben thought about it, the more examples he could pinpoint where he should have taken a stand.

"People don't want to follow meek individuals who shy away from responsibility and they won't put their fate in the hands of someone who comes across as hesitant to take the helm. They want to be led by a person who appears to believe in themself, the team, and the goals set forth. They want to know the leader will not flee when things look bleak. You don't need to be quite as self-assured as Batman, but you gotta show you're in control of the situation. Does this make sense, Ben?"

Ben was still processing how he had messed this up. Hopefully it wasn't too late.

"This leads us to our first Leadership Power," Chief said.

Ben was so wrapped up in the conversation he had forgotten about the Powers.

"Your success is rooted in how committed you are to being accountable for the outcome."

"That is certainly a different mindset," Ben said.

"It can be. Most people are promoted to leadership because they were great at their job; however, it's rarely considered that the skills to be a great individual performer are not the same as being a great leader of individual performers."

"How do you mean?" Ben asked.

"As the lone gunslinger, you were accountable to yourself. Success was dependent upon how you did your job. Other people might have served as resources, but you had direct control over the output. As the leader, you are accountable to your team and your collective goals. Now, your success is based on how the team performs. There's less control because you're relying on others to do their jobs."

"So it's not too late for someone who has been in the leadership role for, let's say, four months, right?" Ben asked with a hopeful tone.

"Depends," Chief said matter-of-factly.

"I was hoping for something more encouraging."

"Well, it depends on the damage being done, the leader's attempts to correct the relationship, and how forgiving the team can be. Any one of those things will determine whether the relationship is beyond repair. But this doesn't mean you shouldn't try. Am I right?"

"You're right," Ben said. "I know you're right."

"Building up your confidence takes time and experience, both within yourself and in how others view you. Don't feel discouraged if your first attempt doesn't work. No leader starts with a team's unconditional support."

"So how can I show I'm committed to being accountable?"

"You've gotta show you're secure in their role. There are a bunch of ways you can do this. One is to hire and promote the best people. If this sounds basic, I agree; employing the top people seems like an obvious decision. However, on an emotional level, it takes a leader with self-assurance to bring on someone who is capable of being better than the leader. When Batman invites someone onto his team, he knows he needs to train them to be the best possible crime-fighter they can be. Otherwise, they would become a liability to themself, the person who needs saving, and other members of the team. The workplace is no different. Leaders must rely on others to be successful. If they are only training people to accomplish the bare minimum, performance will suffer thus negatively impacting the team, the customer, and the organization."

"So I need to hire my replacement?"

"Well said. You want to surround yourself with the highest caliber people you can find. If you're a good leader, you'll get credit for the team's output. Then, when you get the next promotion, your successor is ready to take over."

"Well," Ben said, "I don't have any openings, but I get your point."

"It's not just for the newbies. Confident leaders are secure enough to harness the abilities of their team. They are willing to share high-level information in the interest of developing the skills and mental aptitude of those under their tutelage. The leader is then freed up to serve as a ringleader instead of feeling the need to weigh in on every detail. They can then focus on more strategic ideas while remaining available to support the team."

Chief looked away to wave to another departing customer.

"Okay, Ben. I gave you an example; now you give one to me. What can a leader do to exhibit their confidence?"

"They can--"

"One correction, if I may. Start with 'I' can."

"All right. *I* can," Ben stated, "give away credit when someone does something great."

"But won't others think you weren't doing your job if a team member gets the accolades?" Chief said, playing the devil's advocate.

"Everyone knows that as the leader, I play an integral part in a project's success. I don't need to pat myself on the back. I'm better off singing the praises of the team members' accomplishments. If I didn't begin the project with a team member's support, these actions might increase the chances they'll have a different view of me next time we work together."

"Before we end the night's lesson, I need to give you a warning about confidence," Chief said. "Confidence is often mistaken for being egotistical or conceited. It can be a thin line between believing in yourself and feeling superior to others. I call this the Kingpin Complex. Wilson Fisk, aka the Kingpin, is a feared and powerful crime lord in the world of Spider-Man and Daredevil. He commands a large syndicate of New York

City gangs with a wake of bodies to show for it. Kingpin rules his unlawful empire with determination, brashness, and ambition. Unfortunately, many confuse his bravado for assuredness."

"I haven't shown enough confidence in the past. Now you're saying I'm in danger of showing too much?" Ben asked.

"It's a valid concern. Where self-assurance is displayed through poise and confidence, Kingpin demonstrates his authority through arrogance. He has an exaggerated sense of self-importance, insensitivity to others, frequent displays of self-congratulatory bragging and is basically a bit too full of himself, not to mention his nasty habit of killing people. Self-assured leaders are secure in themselves, whereas leaders like the Kingpin need to feel better than everyone else. If you maintain a sense of humbleness, you'll be okay."

"That shouldn't be a problem. I'm feeling pretty humble right now."

"You are looking a bit worn out. Let's pick this back up tomorrow evening. Two quick things. First, you made a pledge this afternoon that you would practice what you learned. You still committed to this?"

"Without a doubt."

"Good, I'm trusting you'll apply it. This conversation has been great, but experiencing the Leadership Powers is the only way to truly learn them. Secondly, your goal tomorrow is to be Spider-Man and Batman."

Chief handed Ben another stack of books to read as he headed out the door.

When Ben got in the car, he heard R.E.M. on the radio singing, "I am, I am, I am Superman, and I can do anything...."

What a way to end the day.

The First Power

THE POWER OF ACCOUNTABILITY

Your success is rooted in how committed you are to being accountable for the outcome.

4

Take Responsibility for the Responsibility

When Ben woke up the next morning, his head was swimming with ideas on ways to exhibit his newfound sense of accountability. Should he make a grand entrance? Could he get a marching band on such short notice?

Ben chose a more subtle approach. Instead of swinging in like Spider-Man, he decided to be cool and collected like Batman. After arriving at the office, he did a walk-around to say good morning to the team. He hadn't done this since his first week. It felt good to start the day with some casual conversation before the crises began.

Ben had been reflecting on the previous day and what issues could have been avoided. There was a ton of preparation needed for next week's meeting with T. Thomas Tylerson; however, before Ben got swept up in a marathon brainstorming session, one bit of unnecessary chaos from yesterday needed to addressed.

Ben had been having issues with his assistant, Betty, for quite some time. In addition to incorrectly setting his calendar and not making him aware of Tylerson's attendance in yesterday's meeting, last month when he was on a business trip, she sent the car service to his hotel at two o'clock in the morning to bring him to the airport. Not only was it the wrong time, but it was the wrong day and the car was at the wrong hotel in the wrong city. The one correct detail was Ben's cell phone number, which the driver continuously called until Ben was wide awake.

When Ben had last attempted to discuss these blunders, Betty started crying before he could get to the point. After this, Ben rationalized that it would get better on its own. This approach seemed easier than trying to have a conversation.

Yesterday's gaffe was the tipping point. One instance is a mistake; this had become a pattern. Batman would never tolerate this, and neither could Ben.

When Betty walked into Ben's office, she looked concerned. It had gotten around that she'd messed up the previous day's meeting. As she was sitting down, she started to explain.

Betty usually sought to take control of these conversations and, before yesterday's session with Chief, Ben had allowed this. Today, he was going to be the leader and take responsibility for the meeting.

Before Betty could get into her tangent, Ben stopped her.

"Betty, we need to talk."

Ben walked her through yesterday's events and described how her mistakes affected him, the department, and the organization. Whereas before he would have backpedaled when it became uncomfortable, this time Ben stood firm. When Betty tried to change topics, he brought it back to this subject. When she tried to blame others, he emphasized the importance of her role and responsibilities.

As the conversation continued, Ben was feeling more and more confident. Because he had taken charge, there was no need to feel defensive. He didn't even raise his voice. Ben wanted this to be constructive; there was no need to be insulting or petty.

"I am accountable for the outcomes of this department," Ben said. "If someone on this team is not pulling their weight, I am doing them a disservice by not addressing it. I think you're capable of more and I want to give you the opportunity to do a better job."

The rest of the meeting was a breeze. Betty described how she's been feeling overwhelmed and disorganized. They came to some workable solutions and decided it would be helpful to meet on a more regular basis.

In the end, Ben couldn't believe how well it went. Betty had thanked him and even given him a hug on her way out. Time would tell whether the new behaviors would endure, but they were off to a good start.

"This must be how Batman feels," Ben thought.

An hour later, Ben received a text from James: "Was just walking by your assistant's desk. She stopped me to apologize for your tardiness yesterday. Said it was her fault and it won't happen again. Gotta love the Power of Accountability."

Ben smiled and continued with his meeting.

5

The Power of Conviction

When Ben arrived at Blaze Comics, he was ready for the next lesson. Since his meeting with Betty, the day had spiraled into an abyss of frustration. His team had made little headway on the Gulag campaign. They were still going in too many directions and this was eating up what little time they had left.

As Ben walked through the door, he heard the now-familiar laser gun. Olsen, the guy debating Chief the previous afternoon, was standing there like he'd been waiting to greet Ben.

"Hey man, sorry about interrupting your conversation yesterday with Chief," Olsen said. "I know he can get pretty deep and I didn't mean to encumber whatever knowledge was being exchanged."

"Don't worry about it. We had barely begun."

"Great. Did Chief mention anything about what makes someone a superhero?"

Before Ben could respond, Chief swept in and ushered Ben away.

"Come on, Chief. Throw me a bone," Olsen bawled as Chief raced Ben across the store.

"He's so close to figuring it out on his own. Giving him the answer would take away his sense of pride...and I do enjoy watching him strain," Chief said with a mischievous grin. "I'm having some fun with him right now, but you should know Olsen is a really talented young man. His storytelling is phenomenal. If you don't mind, I'm going to invite him over to join us in a little bit."

"Sure," said Ben. Having someone else in the discussion might take some pressure off.

"So when we last spoke, you were off to practice the Power of Accountability. How'd it go?"

"I think it went well. I spoke to someone on my team who had been making mistakes. While she was responsible for her errors, I had not been taking responsibility for the department. Basically, by not acting like the leader, I was allowing it to happen."

"Wonderful," Chief said. "Those critical conversations are too often ignored. How'd your newfound confidence affect the rest of your day?"

"It helped, but it wasn't the end-all solution I was hoping for."

"How so?"

"I was leading a big brainstorming session with the team and it was all over the place. I projected confidence and spoke with more certainty, but the team just couldn't focus on a single course."

"Before you get too frustrated, keep in mind that we have four more leadership superpowers to cover. If it only took one, it would be too easy," Chief said. "Anyway, having confidence, in and of itself, does not make someone a leader. The world is full of people who think highly of themselves but lack the ability to channel their self-assurance into action, let alone being able to get others to buy into their plan. Just look at Booster Gold."

"I'm not familiar," Ben said.

"That's okay; Booster is not one of the bigger superhero names. He's an athlete from the 25th century who traveled back to the 20th century to become a hero. Booster had the desire and physical abilities to be a superhero. Yet, with all of his swagger, he was motivated by a vapid, self-seeking goal of being regarded as a great superhero versus actually behaving like one. What Booster and many leaders need to understand is that it's not enough to stand in front of a crowd and declare their leadership."

"Like I did today?"

"Listen, you took the first step and that's a big deal. Now we need to generate some momentum and grow support behind you." Chief then yelled to Olsen, "Hey Jimbo, can I borrow you for a minute?"

Olsen walked over like a teacher ready to lecture his class. He was dressed in faded jeans, a brightly colored t-shirt with some superhero-like emblem, and a worn wool blazer. He was fairly young and wore glasses whose thickness clearly indicated how much time he spent staring at a computer screen.

"What can I do for ya'?" Olsen said.

"As my resident expert on discrimination, would you mind explaining the Professor's school of thought to Ben?"

"Happily," Olsen replied. "Ben, I want you to picture a world where individuals are persecuted because they are different from everyone else. Whether it's because of skin color, the way they speak, or the inherent ability to shoot fire out of their eyes, they are treated as outcasts--"

"Wait, what?"

"They are treated as outcasts?"

"No, the part before that. Did you say the ability to shoot fire out of their eyes?" Ben asked.

"Yeah, these poor souls are ostracized by family members, co-workers, and strangers. They cannot make friends, nobody will hire them, and they are having problems finding a place to live. As tensions escalate, daily rallies are held to protest their integration into society, law enforcement pushes for them to 'register' with the government, news commentators are advocating that they wear an insignia so as to identify themselves, and giant robots are mercilessly hunting them down--"

"I'm sorry. Robots? I thought you were talking about civil rights," Ben said.

"He is," replied Chief. "We're talking about the civil rights of mutants. Sorry for the interruption, Olsen. Please continue."

"Thank you," Olsen said with a playful sneer. "As I was saying, to intervene against this mounting prejudice, a leader emerges. Professor Charles Xavier, a world-renowned geneticist, launches an international movement to encourage equal rights for mutants. His intent is to show that while mutants may appear to be different, they can be constructive, law-abiding members of society."

"Well done. I told you he was a good storyteller," Chief said as he redirected the conversation to Ben. Olsen smiled and walked back to the other side of the store.

"Professor Xavier offered what every leader must be able to provide: guiding principles that can improve the society in which we are living. That is a vision, and every superhero and leader has gotta have one."

"I'm not clear on how a vision helps. Isn't everyone in an organization moving towards a common goal?" Ben asked.

"Only if someone has established what that goal is. Before we get too far along, let's define vision. I like the description from Warren Bennis and Burt Nanus, two of my favorite business-research gurus. They describe it as 'a mental image of a possible and desirable future state.' It expresses a condition significantly better than what currently exists."

"It sounds kinda idealistic, don't you think?"

"Absolutely. It's also ambitious and inspiring. A good vision binds people together. When people share a common vision, they become connected and a bond is created. Believing mutants can be valuable members of society, Professor Xavier used his vision to rouse a team of loyal followers called the X-Men who share his ideals and fight to uphold them. Before this, those in the X-Men had nothing in common expect they were different from everyone else. Your team is the same."

"I wouldn't call my team a bunch of mutants, but I get where you're coming from. I need to provide more direction."

"Yes, but I want you to think bigger. Direction is important, without question, but it's not the same as a vision. By itself, direction is short-sighted."

"Short-sighted?" Ben thought, "Never heard that before."

"Direction points the way you need to go, but it does not attach any meaning or purpose to your actions. If the Professor only gave direction, the X-Men would fight whatever adversary was in front of them. But what happens when they are knocked off-course? Unless the Professor is right there to realign and put them back on track, the X-Men have the potential to do a lot of needless damage. Thankfully, the Professor provides a solid vision that frames how all of the X-Men make decisions. It acts like a bulls-eye to focus efforts. The X-Men use the vision to guide their work, prioritize tasks, and link projects to the 'greater good.' Since they all understand it and believe in it, the Professor's vision is then carried out even when he's not there to enforce it. You with me?"

"I think so. You are saying I need to paint a picture of how I want the team to see the world," said Ben.

"Wow, it sounds overwhelming when you say it like that, but you get the gist. How's about we start a little smaller. Can you describe how you want your department to look in a year?"

"Like a fantasy of how I want it to look?" asked Ben.

"Not quite. A vision is not a dream. It's a carefully formulated idea for the future – a reality yet to materialize. It may resemble a fantasy in that you are visualizing an ideal outcome, but it'll never work if it's based entirely on your imagination. It must be grounded in reality with a road map to identify the building blocks necessary to attain this desired state. So describe how you want your department to look in a year."

Ben started to get anxious. He'd been so focused on the next emergency that he hadn't considered the bigger picture items.

"Relax," Chief said. "You don't have to answer right now. Mull it over. It's a good exercise to get you thinking more long-term. As you consider it, remember that a strong vision compels people to be part of it because they want to, not because they feel they have to. Professor Xavier does not force his colleagues to fight, even though he's one of the most powerful telepaths in the world and is capable of bending anyone's mind to his will. He relies on the power of the vision. Those who do not subscribe to the vision can decide whether they want to go somewhere else."

"That's what I'm worried about," said Ben. "I cannot afford a mass exodus."

"Well, there's the classic metaphysical quandary, 'If a leader sets a vision and no one's around to hear it, did the leader make a sound?'"

Ben ignored Chief's pun. He was concerned whether he'd be able to get buy-in for his vision, whatever that vision may be.

"To build support for your vision," Chief continued, "involve others in developing it. As the leader, you need to facilitate the conversation and put the final stamp on it. This does not mean you should create it in a bubble. I would hate to see you become another Ozymandias."

"Ozymandias?"

"Yeah, Ozymandias. From *Watchmen*? Classic comic book. Anyway, he earned a reputation as the smartest man on the planet. Being the brilliant individual he was, Ozymandias understood that without his intervention, the world powers were on a path to destroy each other through nuclear war. In response, he devised an intricate plan to bring about world peace."

"Sounds like a bold vision," said Ben.

"It was. And Ozymandias successfully carried it out. The downside was that he did not involve anyone else in the planning or execution of his strategy."

"But it worked. He had a clear vision and saw it through. How could there be a downside?"

"Did I forget to mention how he accomplished his vision? To achieve an international cease-fire, Ozymandias united the world behind a fabricated enemy. He killed millions of innocent people, according to him, 'to save billions.'"

"That's awful. You don't consider him to be a superhero, do you?" Ben asked.

"Interesting question. While he was certainly on shaky moral ground, his intentions were benevolent. We will discuss ethics in a sec. For now, let's focus on how he developed his vision. Ozymandias was aware of the controversial nature of his plot, so he did not discuss it with anyone until it was virtually over. He was so secretive that he murdered the superheroes, his old teammates and friends, who got too close to figuring it out. But what if Ozymandias had discussed it with some other people? He may have been highly intelligent, but he also had some sensible, shrewd associates. Maybe as a group, they could have figured out a different way to attain world peace without the bloodshed. We'll never know."

"Got it. I will develop a vision that does not result in massive fatalities," Ben said.

"Instead of saying 'I will develop,' try 'We will develop,' stated Chief. "As the leader, you need to take advantage of the resources around you and utilize the knowledge of your team members. Remember, it's the team's vision, not just yours."

"You mentioned ethics before," Ben said.

"I did, I did. Once you declare your willingness to accept the responsibly of being a leader and you've defined a vision for what you're trying to achieve, you need to determine how you intend to achieve it. This leads us to our next Leadership Power, the Power of Conviction:

Your value is determined by the goals you strive for and the manner in which you achieve them.

Chief leaned back with a smile.

Ben repeated it. "My value is determined by the goals I strive for and the manner in which I achieve them."

Chief nodded. "We've discussed the first part – you've determined the goals through your vision. But the way you achieve these goals is just as important as what you are trying to achieve. We were talking about the X-Men, so let's stick with them. One of the most famous X-Men is Wolverine. Long before joining this team he was raised with his half-brother, Sabretooth."

"They must have some pretty sick parents to names their kids Wolverine and Sabretooth," Ben joked.

"They're nicknames, but it describes them better than their real names. Anyway, Wolverine and Sabretooth were both mutants with animalistic superhuman abilities. They grew up in the same house, possess similar abilities – rapid healing,

49

exceptionally acute senses, and razor-sharp fangs and claws – and have parallel personalities that include a short fuse, a celebration for vengeance, and a fair amount of bloodlust. What differentiates them is how they choose to use their powers. Wolverine exercises a moral code that implores him to help others, while Sabretooth chooses to give in to his bestial nature, thus ruthlessly destroying everything in his path. Same powers, but how they are applied and the intentions behind them distinguish the superhero from the supervillain."

"Isn't this what you and Olsen have been debating?"

"Precisely. And what was the secret formula?"

"Courage," said Ben.

"That's right. When we are discussing ethics, it's the courage to do the right thing."

"How is this courage?" asked Ben.

"Because when you have power, whether it be superpowers or the power that comes from a leadership position, it's easy to get selfish. It's easy to get absorbed in the glamor. It's easy to abuse the advantages associated with the status."

"That would not happen to me," Ben said.

"Do you think corrupt leaders know they're corrupt? Most have perfectly logical justifications for their unethical acts."

"So how do I avoid this?"

"By defining your moral parameters early in your leadership career and sticking to them. Otherwise, if you don't understand who you are and where you stand, power will only cloud your viewpoint. Doing the right thing is already engrained in you. If you can declare it, it'll be harder to rationalize when the grey areas come up. What I want you to think about is 'where's your line'."

"My line?"

"Yeah, how far are you willing to go to get what you want? One option is to be a Frank Castle, aka the Punisher. Punisher vowed to spend his life avenging his family after watching a gang of mobsters ruthlessly murder them. He's an angry dude who believes the end justifies the means. Punisher is willing to obliterate everything and everyone standing in his way to stop the bad guys. He has no reluctance to kill people in the name of justice and will resort to kidnapping, torture, and extortion without remorse."

"He doesn't sound like a superhero to me."

"That's fair. Many other superheroes would agree with you. But Punisher is still defending us from the criminals. He's simply doing it in a more violent way than his costumed colleagues," Chief said. "In my experience, there are many ethical leaders who utilize a Punisher-esque style. They have a righteous cause and are so driven that they willingly wear blinders, ignoring anything that may distract them from success. They use people when they're needed, discard them when they are a hindrance, lie and break rules if it'll further the cause. And they feel morally justified because achieving their noble objective is all that matters."

"It's no different than Ozymandias killing all those people to avert war. That's not what I think about when I hear the word 'superhero' and I question the ethics of a leader with this mindset," Ben replied.

"I get where you're coming from, Ben. It feels inherently wrong to say it's okay to do whatever needs to be done in order to win. Just look at any number of businessmen who have gone to jail because their greed and ego overpowered their moral compass. But what about the CEO who is trying to save the jobs at his company? Or the social activist who is trying to get food to a desperate village? Does the end justify their means? To save the bulk of the jobs, the CEO may need to lay off a portion of his workforce. And the social activist may have to work with corrupt politicians to gain access and deliver lifesaving supplies to the village. Does getting closer to the end zone excuse doing something that may not feel right?" Chief asked.

"I still think I'd rather fall on the other end of the spectrum," said Ben.

"So the end never justifies the mean," replied Chief. "That's fine, too. Since we were talking about the Professor Xavier's X-Men, let's discuss his lieutenant, Scott Summers, aka Cyclops. Cyclops believes some choices cannot be rationalized no matter how morally defensible the consequences. He lives by an ethical code where the motives of himself and his team are equally as important as the results of their actions. It's not enough just to fight side by side; Cyclops wants to win the 'proper way' and commands his team to behave accordingly."

"This sounds more like me," said Ben.

"There is something to be said about focusing on the actions that lead to the outcome. If the goal is to win and the leader does it in a way that deviates from the current ethical norms, the bar has been lowered, which means now everyone can abide by the same sunken standards. The Punisher thinks it's okay to kill mobsters, but because he has justified murder, his successor may decide jaywalkers present the same risks to society and deserve the same punishment."

"Right," said Ben. "The leader sets the precedent for how everyone else should behave."

"True, but the leader is also responsible for the bigger picture. This may not always seem fair to the individuals affected, but there is something to be said about protecting the common good. By the way, did I mention Cyclops' focus on taking 'appropriate' action led to his girlfriend killing him?"

"No," Ben said. "I think you missed that part."

"Well, Jean Grey was a powerful mutant who was possessed by an entity called Phoenix. Phoenix was as malicious as it gets and was virtually unstoppable. Through Jean, Phoenix was destroying everything within eyeshot." Chief stopped and stared at Ben, waiting for a reaction.

"Get it? Eyeshot? Cyclops shoots lasers out of his eyes? My humor is wasted on you. Anyway, Cyclops knew he couldn't kill Phoenix without also killing Jean. When he was finally able to get close enough, he hesitated. Instead of doing what he needed to do to save humanity from this evil being, Phoenix vaporized him. While superheroes don't generally condone killing the bad guy, wouldn't Cyclops have prevented further destruction by this simple act of justifiable homicide? How many lives would he have saved? It's an ethical quandary."

"I'm confused. Are you saying I should be ends-driven like Punisher or means-driven like Cyclops?"

"Yes."

"What do you mean by 'yes'?" Ben asked.

"They are both important. Weighing these two schools of thought is a necessary exercise that'll prepare you for the unforeseen dilemmas. However, instead of picking one of these options, I'd like to propose a third. WWCMD."

"WWCMD?"

"What Would Captain Marvel Do?"

"Captain Marvel? I'm not familiar with him," said Ben.

"So there's this kid named Billy Batson. He had a difficult childhood, enduring many personal hardships – he lost his parents, was separated from his only sibling, and abandoned by his godparent, who also stole his vast inheritance. Still, Billy remained optimistic, warm-hearted, and altruistic. He was a good kid who wanted to avoid physical altercations, but was also willing to stand up for what was right no matter the personal risks or cost."

"We're still talking about superheroes, aren't we?"

Chief ignored Ben's question and continued. "Based on Billy's irrepressible integrity and positive outlook on life, he was chosen by a powerful wizard to be a champion for good. Now, whenever he says the magic word 'Shazam!,' a mystical lightning bolt transforms him into Captain Marvel, an adult superhero with super-strength, flight, and other powers of mythological heroes. Captain Marvel has the power and strength to have garnered the moniker of 'The World's Mightiest Mortal.' However, as impressive as his superpowers may be, what makes Captain Marvel a paradigm to the superhero community is his exemplary character."

"It's an interesting backstory, but being a 'paradigm for much of the superhero community' seems a bit far-reaching," Ben said. "I thought Superman had that reputation."

"I'm always fascinated by who our idols idolize. What if I told you Superman looks up to Captain Marvel as an ethical mentor? We all need advice at times, and the great Superman has looked to Captain Marvel for guidance when he was not sure where to draw the line. Consequently, Captain Marvel's alter ego has been a huge admirer of Superman since well before gaining superpowers."

"What makes Captain Marvel this pillar of morality?" Ben asked.

"Let me give you an example. In Whiz Comics #25, Captain Marvel is once again battling his nemesis, Captain Nazi."

"Captain Nazi? Really?" Ben said.

"Tell me about it. 'General' Nazi would have sounded much more foreboding," Chief replied with a wink. "Anyway, their fight results in an innocent bystander getting struck with an oar and knocked into the water. Captain Marvel is able to save the unconscious boy named Freddy Freeman, and brings him to the hospital. When he learns the extent of Freddy's injuries, Captain Marvel begs his wizard guardian to heal Freddy. The wizard states that the only way to help Freddy is if Captain Marvel donates some of his powers. Without hesitation, Captain Marvel consents. This result in Freddy not just being saved, but he is now super-powered as Captain Marvel, Jr., thereby joining Captain Marvel in his fight against wrongdoers."

"That is pretty impressive."

"The Power of Conviction. It's the culmination of your character through ethics, morality, and behavior. Like Captain Marvel, leaders must adhere to the idea that it is not enough to have virtuous intentions. These intentions must be put into action. Leaders with character show consistency between what is said and what is done. When faced with a moral dilemma, their actions and reactions are fairly predictable and the rationale behind their decisions are transparent. This consistency fosters the trust of team members. Those who trust their leaders display greater job performance, job satisfaction, and organizational commitment."

"How?"

"When leaders don't have the full trust of those on their team, they project confusing signals. This leads to an unstable environment with excessive energy spent deciphering the leader's true intentions. It can be easily avoided if the leader keeps promises, displays honesty and conducts themself by a clear set of well-defined, publically broadcast ethical standards."

"Makes sense," Ben said.

"You see, character is a choice – a choice between doing what a leader knows to be right, a choice on how the leader will face a challenge, a choice as to whether the leader will rise above their self-interest for the betterment of others. Character means doing the right thing even when the consequences are uncertain and there's not a guarantee that it'll result in a reward. When Captain Marvel saved Freddy, he didn't know how much of his own power he'd be giving up to save Freddy. All Captain Marvel considered was whether it was the right thing to do. He also did not know his sacrifice would be rewarded with a new super-powered ally. As far as he was concerned, the reward was saving a young boy."

"I think I understand. As a leader, my team needs to be aware of my ethical stance so they better understand me and why I make the decisions I do."

"Shazam! I think you got half of it," Chief said.

"What half am I missing?"

"Making your morals known is important, no question about it. However, there's a subset of leaders who cloak themselves in a moral veneer without ever intending to follow an ethical course of action. I call this the Penguin Complex. The world knows Oswald Cobblepot as a high-profile aristocrat who owns Gotham City's popular Iceberg Lounge. The truth is that he's the Penguin, a mobster who operates his trendy nightclub as a cover for his criminal activity. Armed with a reputation for civil service and capable public relations representation, Cobblepot engages in moral hypocrisy where he wants to appear moral without behaving morally."

"To complicate matters," Chief continued, "Cobblepot is also deceptive to his lawless associates. Unbeknownst to them, Cobblepot is an informant to Batman where he provides information on the happenings in Gotham's illicit underworld.

"So he wants society to think of him as an upstanding member of society, he wants the underbelly of society to know him as a ruthless racketeer, and he wants Batman to consider him a trusted source of gossip? Juggling so many ethical personas can't be easy," Ben said.

"Indeed. But how many other leaders use ethics as a marketing tool? How many organizations have fancy missions and visions that spout the moral high ground while their business practices are directly to the contrary?"

"You are so right," Ben said. "Everyone working there sees through the facade and starts to emulate the leader's bad behavior. Plus, when they know the leader is a morality impostor, they follow the leader to the top and happily watch as the leader plummets down. There's no loyalty."

"And that is why it's your responsibility as a leader to be the moral compass, not just look like it."

The Second Power

THE POWER OF CONVICTION

Your value is determined by the goals you strive for and the manner in which you achieve them.

6

Vision Isn't Just A Way To See Through Walls

Ben left the comic book store feeling invigorated. Not yet ready to call it a day, he decided to stop by the office to put his late night energy burst to good use.

When Ben arrived, he found Mary Jane, his top performing account representative, in the conference room practicing the pitch to T. Thomas Tylerson. Not wanting to interrupt, he stood outside. Mary Jane started the presentation, expressed her aggravation through some creative profanity, and started over with a different angle. This happened five times before Ben moved into the doorframe and peered in.

Startled by the unexpected visitor, Mary Jane asked, "What are you doing here in the middle of the night?"

"I could ask you all the same question. How's it going?"

"If you've heard anything I've said in the last two hours, you'd know I've gotten nowhere."

"Sounds like you could use a break. Want to go for a walk?"

Mary Jane grabbed her pad of paper and they started strolling through the office. The conversation began light, but Ben was feeling guilty about how he had spoken to her the prior day.

"I owe you an apology," Ben said. "It wasn't your fault I was late to that meeting and it certainly wasn't your fault that your messages didn't reach me."

"Don't worry about it. I know you were frustrated and stressed," Mary Jane responded.

"I am worried. I have a vision for where I would like to see this department go and I have not done a great job communicating it or, quite frankly, living it. But more than that, I'm worried about losing you on my team."

Thinking about what Chief said about Captain Marvel's character and willingness to sacrifice for others, Ben decided to make the ultimate sacrifice.

"I respect you and enjoy working with you. I will never stop you from exploring or seeking new opportunities," Ben continued. "If you're open to it, I'd like to make a deal. If you'll give me until after the Gulag presentation to make a final decision on transferring to another department, I promise I will do everything within my power to help you go wherever you'd like."

"Wow, I wasn't expecting that, Ben. I appreciate your support. Can I ask what's going to change between pre- and post-Gulag? Winning this account will not magically fix the issues on the team."

"Agreed. This team has gotten off to a bumpy start and I take responsibility for that. My sole focus is getting us back on track."

"That's bold, but shouldn't your sole focus be on the Gulag deal?" Mary Jane asked.

"If my only concern is one presentation to one client, then we'll always be chasing our tail. I'm thinking bigger and more long-term."

Ben and Mary Jane spent the remainder of the night talking about the direction of the department. Ben discussed how he envisioned the future. He offered a vivid description with details of where he'd like to be in three months, six months, and a year, as well as what they'll need to get there.

Then, where he would usually bulldoze his way through the conversation and coerce some agreement, Ben considered the Power of Conviction. Ben listened to Mary Jane's concerns. She talked about her impatience with some team dynamics, many of which predated Ben's ascent to Executive Director. She also gently mentioned her disagreement with some of Ben's decisions.

The more Ben listened, the more he felt Mary Jane was not complaining out of some sense of entitlement or disengagement. In fact, it was just the opposite. She was expressing her passion for the work they do and her dedication to the company.

Ben addressed Mary Jane's issues with honesty and transparency. He could not provide every detail she was seeking, but he didn't try to hide this either. Her frustrations had been bubbling for some time. Ben knew this one conversation would not fix everything, but it felt like a positive step.

Once Mary Jane had vented, they shifted into the vision. This was where the discussion went into high gear. Similar to how they prepared for a sales pitch, one idea spawned another and another. This was Ben's favorite part of his job: when everyone was on the same page, propelling towards a common goal.

"I'm sure Professor Xavier feels the same way when he's leading his team against the forces of evil," Ben laughed to himself. Chief would be so proud.

By the time they left, Mary Jane had corrected some crucial flaws in Ben's initial vision. It was now both more realistic and yet somehow more aggressive. What Ben had intended for a year down the road, Mary Jane convinced him could be accomplished in half the time.

They concluded with Mary Jane agreeing to hold off on making her decision to leave the team. Ben wasn't sure what she was thinking, and that was okay.

Regardless of what was going to happen, Mary Jane was trustworthy and dependable. Even if she'd already decided to transfer, Ben was confident that Mary Jane would put everything she had into their final project together.

Now what could he do to get the rest of the team moving in the same direction?

7

Olsen's Origin Story

When Ben arrived at Blaze Comics the next morning, Olsen was outside waiting for him.

"Morning, Ben. How goes it on this beautiful sunny day? Chief mentioned a big breakfast meeting today with one of his colleagues. He asked whether you'd object to my tagging along."

"Of course not," Ben replied. He felt pretty wiped out from the previous night's powwow and appreciated having someone else to help carry the conversation.

"Thanks," said Olsen. "Do you mind driving? Chief said he'd meet us there."

On the way to the meeting, Ben took advantage of this uninterrupted time with Olsen to probe into Chief's background.

"So how do you know Chief?" Ben asked.

"I've been going to Blaze for a while."

"So he's worked there for a long time?"

"Who? Chief? He doesn't work at Blaze. Well, I guess he kinda does. No, Chief is the owner."

"Chief owns the comic book store?"

"He owns the whole franchise."

Olsen sensed Ben's disbelief. "It's true. Chief started Blaze Comics about twenty years ago. Now there's one in most major cities throughout the country. You've been hanging out in the corporate office."

"Unbelievable. I had no idea," Ben said.

"Yeah, he's owned a bunch of companies through the years."

"Then is Blaze like a hobby for Chief?"

"I'd call it more of a passion than a hobby," said Olsen. "When you speak with him, don't you get the feeling he's doing what he loves? I think of hobbies as being a way to distract us from our day-to-day."

"Kind of like you hanging out in a comic book store, right?" Ben inquired.

"Nah, I go to Blaze for inspiration. It helps with my writing."

"And the stories in comic books inspire you?"

"They do, but I could read the books at home. I go to Blaze to converse with people. It loosens the brain juices. Helps me test new ideas, hone in on the good stuff."

Ben knew just what he meant. That's exactly how he'd felt when he was speaking to Mary Jane last night.

"Comic book stores are a great place to speak with creative people who are totally hypercritical," Olsen continued. "You've heard the insane debates – which superhero can beat Hulk in a fight? Or Flash in a race? Who's the smartest? How does Wonder Woman find her invisible jet? Why does Robin, the Boy Wonder, wear short shorts? The questions are never-ending."

"Aren't all these debates based in conjecture?" asked Ben.

"Aren't all debates based in conjecture to some extent? The comic book crowd are nit-picky readers who meticulously dissect facts and seek out dissent to substantiate their point of view. I try to surround myself with these types of people; they challenge me to be better. It's like Chief says – 'If everybody was satisfied with himself, there would be no heroes.'"

"Chief's quite the philosopher," said Ben.

"Actually, that's Mark Twain," responded Olsen. "Chief just likes sayin' it."

Before Ben could follow up, they arrived at their location.

As they walked into the upscale diner, it was clear to Ben that this was where the power players ate. You could feel the world-altering decisions being made throughout the packed restaurant.

High-level executives were solidifying deals and discussing the day's events over pancakes and eggs. These were certainly not middle managers; Ben would recognize his own kind and they were not here. No, the men and women dining this morning displayed the poise and assurance associated with being in the upper echelon of a successful, global corporation.

As Ben scanned the room hoping to absorb some of its knowledge, he spotted Chief. In a room of high-end suits, Chief stood out in his typical jeans/flannel ensemble. Yet, he displayed the same confidence as the other patrons. "How does he do that?" Ben thought.

When they first walked in, Olsen had been waved over to a table by some friends so Ben made his way through the bustling restaurant by himself. Chief was sitting in the back booth while three men in suits stood over him having an intense conversation. Actually, the three men were intense; Chief seemed relaxed and a bit entertained.

"--and that's why you've gotta dump the stock. It's poison. It won't be worth a quarter of this amount by year's end," the shortest of the three anxiously pleaded.

"We seem to disagree," responded Chief. Seeing Ben, Chief abruptly ended the one-sided argument. "I'm sorry, gentlemen, my guest has arrived. Have a wonderful day and I hope you enjoy your breakfast." Before the three men could turn around to go back to their table, Chief greeted Ben, inviting him to sit down.

"Thanks for joining me this morning," Chief said.

"Thank you for the invitation. This is some place," Ben said, still gawking at his surroundings.

"You like it? When I first entered into the partnership, this was a simple diner with French toast that would melt in your mouth. Strong local following but not enough to afford the rent."

"You own this restaurant?" Ben said in disbelief.

"I have the minorest of a minority stake. Enough to not need a reservation, apparently not enough to get a refill on coffee."

Ben suppressed his surprise. "So what persuaded you to invest in this place?"

"I just told you. It has French toast that melts in your mouth. I never expected it to become the 'in' breakfast spot. We didn't make any significant changes – painted, bought new chairs, nothing fancy. The food spoke for itself. After a few months it somehow caught on."

Ben could not believe how he'd misjudged Chief. When Ben woke up this morning, Chief was but a wise comic book store clerk. A few hours later, Chief's a thriving entrepreneur owning multiple businesses.

"So you said 'we' bought this place. Who's 'we'?" Ben asked.

"I have a few partners. One of them will be joining us shortly. Speaking of guests, where'd Olsen go?"

"He saw someone he knew. Said he'd be back in a minute. Before Olsen gets back, what's his deal?" Since Ben was so wrong about Chief, maybe he was wrong about Olsen too. After all, Olsen had friends amongst this distinguished crowd and had asked Ben to order him the number two with an extra order of bacon, not an order for a first timer.

"How do you mean, 'What's his deal'?"

"Well, I originally thought he was just some guy who hung around your store. This morning, I'm not completely trusting my ability to form an accurate first impression."

Chief explained that Olsen and his mom had moved here when Olsen was in high school. He was a shy kid with an affinity towards comic books and a natural storytelling ability. Olsen spent his afternoons in Blaze and his evenings writing. He won a few local 'young author' contests and eventually went to college on a full scholarship.

Whenever Olsen was home from school he continued to stop in the store. Every time, he'd replenish his comic book collection and leave Chief with samples of his work. Once he graduated, Olsen moved back to the area to pursue his dream of becoming a professional writer.

"What kind of stuff does he write?" asked Ben.

"Depends. He's written a few articles that were published in national magazines, been the ghostwriter on a few novels, and has a weekly blog on a news site. But Olsen's dream is to develop a superhero. He'll get there. Like I said, he's a talented writer."

Ben made a note to check out some of Olsen's stuff when he got into the office.

"Even when he was a kid," Chief said, "what I've always admired about Olsen's writing is his concentrated effort to transact, transform, and transcend."

"Transact, transform, and transcend?" Ben interrupted. "That could be the slogan of a marketing campaign."

"No doubt," agreed Chief. "Olsen uses these three T's to determine the angle for his stories, but they're equally applicable to leaders. *Transact* – an exchange of work product for a reward. *Transform* – motivating the team through a common goal. And *transcend* – giving team members what they need so they can determine and attain the goals."

Ben thought about how he'd been leading his team. There wasn't a whole lot of transcending taking place.

"All too often," Chief said, "leaders depend on transacting. The problem is that once you start relying on tangible incentives, you'll have to give them something every time you want a little extra effort. 'I deserve more money to do this,' someone will say, 'because you gave it to me last time.' The drive to achieve is replaced with entitlement."

"So transforming is better," Ben hesitantly stated.

"You're no longer bribing them, which is a step up. But the leaders who make the greatest impact both professionally and personally are those whose focus is on transcending. Instead of a leader-centric approach, the emphasis is more team-centric. The leaders are still the drivers of the vision, but once it's established, their role is to help others perform to the best of their abilities. It's not 'What can I get out of my staff?' but 'How can I be of assistance?'."

"Why is this 'transcending'?" asked Ben.

"Because you, the leader, are transcending beyond your self-interests to meet the needs of the team and its members. If you consistently approach people and problems with this mindset, you'll be seen as a selfless, trusted ally in all facets of your life."

"In all facets? Really?" This seemed overstated.

"You don't think people are more receptive to a caring, self-sacrificing persona versus a self-centered egomaniac who's only looking out for himself?"

"Well, when you put it like that."

Chief smiled and continued with the story of Olsen.

A few years ago, Olsen was working on a column for one of the larger news magazines. He was unknown and fresh out of college. For whatever reason, one of the owners of the magazine insisted that Olsen be featured. Understandably, the editor was not thrilled to have an unknown writer pushed on him, but he relented after reading a few of Olsen's samples. Even back then, Olsen had a unique writing style with comedy blended into powerful social commentary.

The editor appreciated Olsen's talents but was still hesitant so he assigned a topic that Olsen quickly recognized as filler – it could take up space if the magazine could not "fill" the advertising space. Nonetheless, Olsen saw the opportunity and devoured it. Like a man obsessed, he churned out a two-page opus within the week.

The editor was impressed and, even without the mandate from his boss, was leaning towards finding space in the upcoming publication for Olsen's piece. However, the article was not perfect. The editor delivered some biting criticism and said it was way too long. To ease the pain, he hinted that after completing these edits, Olsen should expect to make more money on his next article.

Being so new to the profession, Olsen took these critiques a little too personally and refused. This was not out of entitlement; Olsen was completely unaware that the editor felt pressured to include his work. And it wasn't about the money; he was earning enough to make a living as a writer even if the bills most months were tight. No, Olsen considered himself an artist.

"So Olsen says to the editor--"

"--this is an affront to my artistic integrity," Olsen howled as he walked towards Ben and Chief's table. "I don't know why you find such joy in telling this embarrassing story, Chief."

After a few witty jibes at each other, Chief continued.

A few days passed and the editor received a call from the owner strongly encouraging the editor to try again. When the editor contacted Olsen this time, he recognized the need for a different approach; offering more money was not to going to work. So appealing to Olsen's artistic side, the editor explained that the magazine was revamping its entertainment section and Olsen's piece would serve an integral role in the new design.

The editor could sense he was getting closer to convincing Olsen, but wasn't quite there. His request still had a "what can you do for me" feel. It was then that the editor asked the single most important question a leader can pose: "What do you think?"

Up until now, the editor had attempted to *transact* with more money and *transform* with his vision of the magazine, but he hadn't *transcended*. By saying, "What do you think?" the editor was finally opening up the dialogue.

The editor and Olsen spent the rest of the afternoon in vibrant conversation. They discussed the direction of the magazine, how media was changing, and on and on. By the end of the day, they had a completed article that both agreed was better than the original draft. Additionally, the editor had some new ideas for the magazine's revamp and Olsen was able to submit his work as a featured columnist.

"The funny thing was that the editor was never forced to hire Olsen. When Olsen's samples were sent, the note simply said, 'Check this out.' He inferred the rest." Chief chuckled.

"Wait, how do you know what was written on the note?" Ben asked.

"Oh look," Chief interrupted, "our breakfast guest is here."

8

The Power of Persuasion

Before Ben could fully comprehend Chief's bombshell, he locked eyes with the fourth member of today's breakfast cohort. Maneuvering with ease through the crowded restaurant was James, the vice president of Ben's division.

Ben smiled and shook his head. He couldn't keep up with all the surprises he'd stumbled upon this morning.

When James sat down, he gently rested a pot of steaming coffee on the end of their table. "Morning, gentlemen," he said with his typical lighthearted charisma, "anyone need a refill? The food is great but they treat coffee like a precious commodity."

"You should do something about that," Chief joked "Ownership should have some privileges."

Without giving Ben time to react, Chief continued, "Let me introduce you to Olsen, the young man I was telling you about."

"Nice to finally meet you," James said. "I'm a big fan of your work." James then redirected the conversation back to Chief. "Seriously, how long have you been waiting for a server to come to the table? If a big shot like you can't get more coffee, what are the chances for everyone else?"

Without warning, James stood up with his carafe of coffee and walked from table to table offering patrons refills. He didn't get through more than three tables before a waitress approached him. Ben didn't need to hear what was being said; the look on James' face was eerily similar to the one he wore when he and Ben had their chat a few days ago. Seeing it as a bystander, Ben noticed that the expression was an interesting blend of serious and stern with caring and concerned.

"I know I'm a 'silent partner' in this place, but I've never been good at not talking," James said when he came back to their booth.

"You have many virtues, my friend, but silence has never been one of them," Chief joked. "Would you mind sharing with the table why you didn't yell or scold the waitress?"

"Why cause a scene? The service would have improved and we'd all be drinking hot coffee right now, but those effects would be short-lived. My approach served three purposes. One, people needed their morning caffeine fix. Two, by serving the coffee I was making a statement that I'm not above doing the grunt work. The exhibition was a bit passive-aggressive but I needed to get her attention."

"A bit?" Chief joked.

"Fine, it was completely passive-aggressive," James said smiling, "but the follow up conversation was clear and to the point. My third purpose in handling it the way I did was I don't want an Otis-filled restaurant."

"Otis-filled?" Ben asked.

"Yes, a restaurant full of people who act like Otis. You see, the art of leadership lies in the way leaders motivate their team. Lex Luthor has much to teach us about this."

"Lex Luthor?" Ben asked. "Wait, you're into superheroes, too?"

"Technically, Lex is a supervillain."

"So you want me to be more like Lex?" This was a lot for Ben to take in.

"No, often the best lessons are what *not* to do. In that respect, supervillains like Lex have as much to teach us about leadership as the heroes. In regards to motivation, Lex doesn't concern himself with instilling inspiration or encouragement because he surrounds himself with weak-minded people, like his henchman Otis, whom he can order around. Otis attempts to follow Lex's instructions but he is not permitted to solve even the most minor problems on his own. Hence, he persistently messes up Lex's plans for world domination."

"Can't it be argued," Olsen interjected, "that Otis messes up Lex's plans because he lacks the mental fortitude to carry out the jobs assigned? He is characteristically a bumbling, dim-witted manservant."

"Is he," replied James, "or is this just how Lex treats him? I would argue that Otis' persistent blundering is to be expected. How would you feel if your boss repeatedly said things to you like, 'It's amazing that brain can generate enough power to keep those legs moving?' When everything you do ends in an insult, how long before confidence is chiseled away?"

"So you're saying Otis has the potential to be a top performer?"

"I'm saying we'll never know if Lex doesn't give him a chance. Right now, Lex leads Otis through bullying and micromanagement. Admittedly, this brand of leadership is easy; however, it is not effective in generating the most or best work from others. In a nutshell, if you treat people like idiots, they're going to act like idiots. It's the leader's responsibility to raise the expectations."

James then looked at Ben. "That's what I meant when I said I don't want an Otis-filled restaurant. I want independent thinkers who are self-propelled to do great work, and I need leaders who treat them as such."

After the server came to table, thanked James for his assistance, and took their breakfast order, the foursome continued with some light banter before Chief got back to business.

"I didn't just invite James to join us this morning because of his table-waiting skills," Chief kidded, "He's here because I don't know anyone who better personifies the Power we'll be discussing today. Olsen, would you mind setting the mood with some backstory on *Sub Diego*?"

"My pleasure. A while back, San Diego suffered a devastating earthquake that plunged half the city into the ocean. Expecting to find massive fatalities, the world was surprised to discover that people had survived the catastrophe by somehow gaining the ability to breathe underwater. Understandably, these individuals were terrified and confused. Panic consumed these victims as they fought to get to the surface where they quickly suffocated when trying to breathe air."

"We're back to talking comic books, right?" Ben confirmed.

Olsen ignored Ben's question. "Thankfully, Aquaman saw people in need and took action. He brought a sense of calm to the inhabitants and foresaw a new direction for the city, newly named 'Sub Diego.' However, this did not come easy. When he first arrived, Aquaman tried to coerce the subaquatic survivors into remaining under the water. Being the King of the Seven Seas, he was not used to people questioning his commands or refusing to listen to him. Aquaman uses telepathic abilities to compel marine life to do his bidding. He commands a kingdom covering three-fourths of the Earth's surface, including Atlantis. And he's well known as the predominant ocean-based superhero. Why wouldn't an aimless group of novice ocean-dwellers blindly follow his directives?"

Olsen took a bite of his French toast before he continued.

"Aquaman barked orders to get people to start rebuilding their city. When they continued their attempts to flee the water, he had sharks serve as guards. His vision was to save them and create an underwater community; why couldn't they see this and be instantly inspired? Once Aquaman realized his style wasn't effective, he changed course. Aquaman started selling his vision for Sub Diego instead of forcing it upon the populace. It was at this point when he transformed from warden to leader."

Chief looked at James and said, "I told you he's an excellent storyteller." He then looked back at Ben.

"This leads us to our next Power, the Power of Persuasion:

Your effectiveness is based on your ability to influence others.

79

"James," Chief said, "let's start with you. When you spoke to the coffee scrooge, why didn't you just tell her to get people their coffee?"

"Because I don't adhere to the customary idea that the role of a leader is to get others to do what they would not otherwise do."

"Isn't that exactly what leaders are supposed to be doing?" asked Ben.

"I prefer to think of leaders as those who motivate people to do more than they originally anticipated and often more than they thought possible. It may initially seem like a subtle difference, but where many choose to lead by pushing people in a direction, my way is centered around you wanting to do it yourself."

"That's the Power of Persuasion," Chief interjected, "It's about *influencing* others, not *commanding* them." Chief then redirected his questioning to Olsen.

"Olsen, for your first magazine column, how did the editor make you write it?"

"Make me? He couldn't make me do anything. He convinced me."

"Exactly," Chief said, "As leaders, we can't make anyone do anything."

"I don't know," responded Ben, "I've had a boss who yelled and barked orders whenever she wanted something done."

"Sounds horrible. Was this boss holding a gun to your head?"

"No."

"Please don't tell me she was holding your family hostage in exchange for your servitude?"

"Of course not."

"So you followed her directive because you choose to," Chief affirmed.

"That's not how it felt at the time."

"No, it probably didn't," James assured him, "but that's what distinguishes leaders from bosses. She and many others use fear to get others to do their bidding. This is so easy, but it's also short-sighted. If fear is your go-to method of motivating, it'll take continuous maintenance. You will need to remind me every day that I'm suppose to be scared."

"And what happens on the day the leader's not in the office?" Chief asked James.

"Someone once said the sign of a great leader is in how followers behave when the leader's not around. If you go on vacation and the whole place falls apart, I question how effective you are."

"Good point," said Chief. "So let me ask you, Ben. There are hundreds of techniques for influencing others. Give me three. Wait, that's too simple, especially for someone like you whose job it is to sell ideas. Give me three techniques that do not involve talking."

Chief saw Olsen snicker at Ben being thrown into the hot seat. "Don't think you're just a spectator for this conversation. For every method Ben says, you owe me a caped-crusading example."

Ben looked around the table as everyone waited for his first example. The pressure was on. He took a sip of coffee to stall.

"To influence others, you need to lead by example?" Ben hesitantly said.

"Why?" asked Chief, prodding for more details.

"I can influence people by the way I act. When I model behaviors, I'm setting an unspoken standard about what is appropriate and what is not. Others will see what I'm doing and, hopefully, try to do it too."

"You're right. We learn about acceptable behaviors by observing those in charge. They set the tone for the whole organization." Chief then looked at Olsen. "You're up."

"Most superheroes serve as archetypes to model the high standards with which we should live our lives."

"Pick one," nudged Chief.

"All right, I'm going with Captain America."

"Besides his strength, agility, and high moral standards, how does Captain America lead by example?" asked Chief.

"Just look at his backstory. In the early 1940s, this scrawny kid is disturbed by the rise of Germany's Third Reich. He attempts to enlist in the Army but he can't pass the physical. Day after day this kid goes back to the recruitment office hoping they'll reconsider. At some point, one of the Army guys recognizes his passion and he gets enrolled in a top-secret defense research program that turns him into the Super-Soldier, Captain America."

"That's an eloquent summarization of seventy years of comics. But how is Captain America leading by example?" peppered Chief.

"It's in his influence over the readers. The first Captain America book came out within the first year of World War II. It showed our protagonist dressed in an American flag-styled costume punching Adolf Hitler in the face. From then on, Cap was a manifestation of patriotism, representing the strong feelings of nationalism that were underway."

"Is it possible you're overstating his importance?" Ben asked. "How can a cartoon character make such an impact?"

"The first issue sold over a million copies and Captain America remained the top-selling comic book through the war. For kids, he provided wish fulfillment. Until he was given his powers, he was just like them. And he wasn't invulnerable; he was just tougher and braver than most. This made him relatable."

"Relatability is another important quality in a leader," Chief interrupted. "Carry on."

"But Cap didn't just speak to the youth. The troops read his books en masse. Not only were they a morale booster, but Cap displayed all the characteristics a real-life 'super-solder' possessed. He led by example, as he was depicted fighting alongside soldiers."

"Nice twist, buddy boy. You could have gone with how Cap was a model for the superhero community, but instead you went with his influence on the country. Bravo. So Ben, what's your second approach for influencing others?"

Ben thought about his late night session with Mary Jane. Besides pitching his vision, what had he done?

"Listening," Ben blurted out. "Leaders need to listen to what other people are saying." Before Chief could ask for more detail, Ben continued, "But you're not just listening for what's being said; you're also witnessing the feelings behind it – tone, body language, emotions."

"And how does listening influence others?" Chief asked.

"How can you influence when you don't know what the other person needs?" Ben thought about Mary Jane again. "And the simple act of paying attention, of giving your time to someone else, validates their importance. You may be trying to collect more information, but they will react by being more receptive to your point of view."

"I like it," Chief said. "And you're right, listening allows you to learn from people and connect with them." He then turned towards Olsen.

"Flash," Olsen confidently stated.

"Flash? The fastest man alive? How does someone who runs faster than the speed of light become the poster-child for listening skills?" Chief asked.

"Because he also thinks at the speed of light. Imagine how much patience it must take to think that fast but be relegated to the snail's pace of the rest of the world. Flash speaks and then has to wait and wait for the reply. It's gotta use every bit of his concentration to focus on what others are saying."

"Very true," Chief nodded, "and, like Flash, since most leaders are thinking at a faster pace, they need to demonstrate the same restraint. Too often, leaders appear to be listening when really they're just formulating the next thing they are going to say. Nicely done. Ben, have you our third?"

"How about personalizing the message?"

"I thought we were going with talkless techniques?" Olsen goaded.

"It does involve speaking, but I'm not referring to what's being said; it's the method of saying it," Ben replied. "Influencing others involves an understanding of people's personalities, needs, and motivations. Then, you can adapt your behavior to increase compatibility."

"That sounds insincere to me. Aren't you just telling people what they want to hear?" asked Olsen.

"Not at all. At work, I have one person who's inspired by the challenge of a new project, whereas someone else needs to hear the financial impact, and another is interested in the big-picture societal aspects. My message doesn't change. I'm simply reframing the ways I communicate it. In the end, they'll all hear the same thing. I just make sure the aspects they care about are included."

"You also need to consider their differing levels of education, attention spans, and the current state of your relationship. If they already trust you, they'll need a lot less convincing than if you just met. That's a solid three," Chief applauded. "Olsen?"

"If you don't mind, I've got one," said James.

"By all means."

"I'd like to go back to the Aquaman Sub Diego storyline. As Aquaman found, ordering people around was not going to influence them to stay with this new underwater community. They were scared about being trapped in this new world and resistant to changing their entire outlook on how to conduct their lives."

"Much of the Sub Diegans' resistance came from under-communication. One conversation would not persuade the populace to change everything they knew; it was going to take multiple methods of communication and repeated attempts before the message truly sunk in. John Kotter, a widely regarded expert on the topic of leadership, suggests leaders estimate how much communication is needed, and then multiply their effort by a factor of ten. The communication must be constant and consistent. It must be emphasized in meetings and trainings. It must be reflected in processes and procedures. It must be quoted by leaders throughout the organization and interwoven in the team's tasks. Then, just when it feels like overkill, add a little more. The idea is to make it part of every individual's subconscious thoughts."

James took a sip of coffee before he continued.

"To gain support, Aquaman did not depend on big speeches, although he did give a few. He spoke to people individually and in small groups. He made it personal by discussing their concerns and fears. Aquaman did not make empty promises about a utopian future, but he did provide the assurance that they were all in this together. A new direction can be scary and, like the citizens of Sub Diego, most people do not welcome change. This does not mean they are incapable of adapting or that they don't understand why the change is necessary."

"So what did Aquaman do once he had the masses on his side?" Chief asked, clearly knowing the answer.

"There were still a few outliers who weren't convinced. Too often, we write off these individuals as troublemakers, disengaged, or disloyal. In reality, they tend to be the informal leaders who have an influential voice around the water cooler."

"Aquaman pun unintended," smiled Olsen.

"In Sub Diego, there were still some who refused to accept they could not return to the air-breathing world. It wasn't until Aquaman individually approached each of the dissenters were they willing to give their new home a chance. Once he had the backing of these informal leaders, Aquaman found he had a whole new layer of supporters."

"Nothing takes the place of a personal touch," Chief added.

"That's why it's your turn to speak with the server about getting us the check," James said with a wink.

The Third Power

THE POWER OF PERSUASION

*Your effectiveness is based on your
ability to influence others.*

9

Selling an Idea is Like Protecting the World From an Alien Invasion...It Takes Effort

When Ben walked into the office after his brunch meeting, he barely had time to put his stuff down before Mary Jane shuffled him into the conference room. Seated before him was every member of his team.

Mary Jane could not contain her excitement. "All right, everyone. I think we've turned a corner with the Gulag campaign. Ben, would you mind going over what we discussed last night?"

"Sure," Ben said. He hadn't expected to have such an immediate opportunity to practice the Power of Persuasion, but he relished the chance.

Taking over the whiteboard in front of the room, Ben outlined the Gulag campaign and T. Thomas Tylerson's critiques; however, he spent most of the time on the vision of the department. He touched on his initial flaws and he took responsibility for the department's shortcomings. Ben was not trying to be self-effacing. He cited his vulnerabilities to demonstrate how these issues would be corrected.

Since Ben had been able to organize his thoughts with Mary Jane the night before, his concepts sounded more eloquent when presented to the team. He avoided a long-winded lecture so everyone would have a chance to ask questions and provide additional feedback. Ben wanted to hear their ideas on how they could accomplish the goals set forth.

Midway through, James walked in. He sat in the back so as to avoid interrupting. When the meeting broke up, James and Ben remained in the conference room.

"Looks promising," James said. "So what's next?"

"What do you mean? I think it went well."

"It did, but not everyone was as bought in as Mary Jane."

Ben could tell by the team's feedback that most of them supported his vision. He also knew that a few were harder to influence. They'd need more convincing.

"Any suggestions on how I can win over the outlying members of the team?" Ben asked.

"A few ways. First, keep the message simple. Aquaman's initial campaign in Sub Diego focused on the items of greatest importance: survival. This was not the time to distract anyone with details; that would come once they fully understood the overarching goal. Personally, I know I've been successful when everyone on my team can recite the vision in less than a minute."

Without thinking, Ben then reeled off the mantra of the division. James had been hammering it into his head for years.

"Exactly," James smiled. "There's no reason why your team should not be able to do the same thing with your vision. The second way is with candor. People can read through the flowery language and false politeness. Be straightforward and honest. Don't sugarcoat the unpleasant parts."

Ben nodded. He knew he'd been guilty of making things sound better than they were. Just ten minutes ago, someone in the meeting had asked about the implications of losing the Gulag account. Ben could have given an answer that more frankly addressed the realities of the situation, but it felt uncomfortable so Ben avoided it.

"It takes time, but you're going in the right direction," James continued. "I haven't seen this many smiling faces in your department for quite some time. There is one more way to persuade the unpersuadable."

Ben sat up. He was eager for whatever advice James had to offer.

"Have the know-how to speak in their language. Say it in a way that will resonate with each individual on the team."

"And how do I do that?" Ben asked, prying for more details.

"By learning the next Power."

10

The Power of Competence

The next day, Ben arrived at Blaze Comics with coffees in hand, a to-go order from the diner, and the comic books he'd been assigned to read. Having last night off gave him time to reflect on all he'd learned thus far. To call it educational would downplay the impact it was having on him.

"Good morning, Chief. Hope you don't mind if we make it a working breakfast. I've been craving the diner since we left yesterday."

Just as Ben held up the bag to show Chief, Chief held up two styrofoam boxes. "I was thinking the same thing," he said as he exploded into laughter. "At least today we won't be in need of coffee."

With their feast on display, Ben began.

"Chief, before we get into it, I cannot tell you how grateful I am for this experience. I feel like I've been reinvented."

"In comics we call this retconning."

"Retconning?"

"As a leader, what happens if you don't change with the times?" Chief asked.

"You become stagnant. Irrelevant. Ineffective."

"It's the same for superheroes. Retconning is when a superhero is altered to keep them relevant. The Daredevil book was on the verge of cancelation until Frank Miller retconned him from the 'sightless swashbuckler' into a ninja-like antihero. Hawkman was a reincarnated Egyptian prince before he was retconned into an alien policeman from the planet Thanagar. Even Lex Luthor went through a major retcon when he was transformed from a mad scientist into an international business mogul."

"What about Flash?" Ben asked. "On the back wall is a poster featuring two versions of Flash. One looks like something out of the 1940s. The other is in the more current red, full-body spandex. It looks like the writer created a whole new look, a new image."

"You're on the right track, Ben. The one piece you're missing is Flash's new persona came with a new person. Jay Garrick was the original Flash. After around ten years, his popularity dwindled so the publisher decided to rethink the character. It was decided that it'd be easier to recast Barry Allen as the 'new and improved' Flash rather than retcon Garrick's dated version."

"So they fired Garrick?" Ben was baffled.

"I never thought of it like that. I guess in some ways they did. By creating a new Flash, they were able to make the character fresh without contradicting the original incarnation. That's tough. While many retcons bring in a new audience, they also run the risk of alienating the original fanbase. It's rare that such an extreme retcon makeover as Barry Allen's Flash is successful; most don't fare so well."

"Don't people want their favorite superheroes to be up-to-date?"

"Sure, but they also don't like change. Especially when it counters everything they know."

Ben felt a surge of inspiration. "What if instead of retconning, the superhero was constantly evolving so there would be no need to retcon?"

"You just blew my mind. Seriously, I love that concept."

"It's kinda like the Oracle book you assigned me to read," Ben continued. "Barbara Gordon was Batgirl until Joker paralyzed her from the waist down and she was no longer able to fight the bad guys."

'Not physically, anyway. Go on."

"So Barbara returned to crime-fighting under the new moniker of Oracle. Instead of directly confronting the criminals as Batgirl, she became the 'information broker' who assisted other superheroes with her intellect and computer savviness. That's a story about evolving. It's about determining what doesn't work anymore and having the flexibility to do something different."

"Maybe a state of continuous evolution is a less extreme form of retconning," Chief added.

"Barbara's conversion into a wheelchair-laden brainiac seemed pretty extreme to me."

"I was actually talking about the leaders' need to continuously change and adapt. You know, it's not always about superheroes," Chief smirked.

"Do you know how Barbara made the shift from Batgirl to Oracle?" Chief asked.

"She recognized the reality of her situation and reinvented herself."

"Well, that's what she did. What's more interesting is how Barbara made the transition from a physical powerhouse into the information hub of the superhero community."

Ben sat up, anticipating the big reveal.

"She did it with the fourth Leadership Power, the Power of Competence:

There is no substitute for being knowledgeable and skilled.

"That's it?" Ben thought. This seemed so obvious. Of course leaders need to be knowledgeable and skilled.

"You're probably thinking this is obvious, right?" Chief said. "You're thinking, 'Of course leaders need to be knowledgeable and skilled.'"

It was eerie how Chief could read Ben's mind.

"As apparent as this may be, you'd be amazed at how many leaders overlook this Power," Chief continued. "They rely on their personality to win support. The importance of substance, however, cannot be dismissed. True leadership doesn't happen without a ton of hard work behind it."

"But I've known plenty of people who were born leaders," Ben said with concern.

"No such thing as a born leader," Chief responded. "This is one of the oldest debates in leadership theory. Mythically, there are these genetically superior individuals who presumably emerge with the ability to lead any group, at any time, under any circumstances. These imaginary leaders have no need to train, for their charisma draws mere mortals to their 'leaderly' glow. Unfortunately, it is rarely this easy."

Ben thought about James. He did not seem to put in any great amount of effort. Instead, he floated through the office without a care in the world.

"Truly successful leaders do not awake with the powers necessary to run a multimillion dollar company, lead a church fundraising committee, or command a brigade of female Amazonian warriors. What might appear effortless is really the culmination of education, experience, and practice. Ultimately, they are so well prepared that they make it look simple. All the confidence and conviction in the world can't change this."

"When you mentioned Amazonian warriors, you were referring to Wonder Woman, right?"

"I was. You might see Wonder Woman as a born leader. She was born into royalty and raised with the expectation that she would succeed her mother as queen. While Wonder Woman could have sat idly by waiting for her seat at the throne, her mother, being the great queen she is, provided extensive training on the skills necessary to lead her island of female warriors."

"It's not like there was an equal opportunity to become the leader of the tribe. It was a monarchy and her reign was a birthright. Wonder Woman would have become the leader without all of the training," Ben said.

"She would have become queen. That does not necessarily mean she would have become the leader. One is a title, the other is a skill. What would have happened if Wonder Woman was thrust into her role without any preparation?"

"She'd be sitting in a comic book shop talking to you?" Ben quipped.

"I could be so lucky." Chief smiled. "What would happen to Wonder Woman is the same thing that happens to any leader not qualified for the job: either you're removed from power or an outside force conquers you and there is no longer power to be had."

To mask his nervous energy, Ben took another long sip of coffee. Those two options were hitting too close to home.

"How did you get promoted to Executive Director?" Chief asked.

"I was an account representative and worked my way up."

"And that is how most people are promoted. But did being a great account representative guarantee you'd be an effective leader? They call for different skill sets, yet we view performance at the subordinate job as a predictor of success for the leadership job."

"Maybe not," Ben responded, "but it was a chance for the executive team to see what I'm capable of. They saw my work ethic, how I fit into the culture of the organization. I had a track record of success and led a few projects before my promotion."

"They clearly saw your leadership potential. I see it too; that's why we're here. But let's shift gears for a second. One of the books I assigned you was Green Arrow. Tell me about him."

Ben went on to explain that Green Arrow is Oliver Queen, a billionaire businessman and CEO of Queen Industries. Queen was a self-centered, egotistical playboy until his yacht capsized and he was stranded on a remote island. With years of seclusion, he was forced to master the bow and arrow. He also had time to reflect on what type of person he wanted to be. When Queen returned to civilization, he chose to use his abilities and resources as the crime-fighter Green Arrow.

"When I hear Green Arrow's story, I always think about the technical skills he acquired to survive on the island. This is a big piece of the Power of Competence – having an understanding of, and proficiency in, specific activities. For Green Arrow, those technical skills led him to become an expert hunter. What other technical skills did he need to develop?"

"The book only focused on his use of the bow."

"You don't actually believe a person can survive on an island by themself for five years with only the ability to fight? One skill set got him through the grueling experience? Seems fictional. How many different jobs are there in your department?"

"Around ten," Ben answered. This felt like a trap, but he had no idea where it was going.

"And, to clarify, you were promoted based on your account representative abilities?"

"I was."

"So what have you done to build your technical skills in the other nine roles?"

"I have qualified professionals who are responsible for and empowered to do their job."

"Then why do they need a leader? If they're so good, shouldn't they know what to do without you directing them?"

"I provide the vision for the team. I barrel through the roadblocks and politics so they aren't distracted. I do the big-picture stuff and bring all the pieces together," Ben said defensively.

"Did I spark a nerve? Listen, you can't be the expert in every job in your department. If you could, then you'd be in a department of one. What I want you to think about is that your promotion was based on mastering the technical skills of one piece of your department. Just as Green Arrow had to grasp a multitude of other skills to endure on the island, your probability of providing meaningful leadership will hinge on your ability to move beyond your primary strength to grasp the other roles of those on your team."

Chief attended to an early-morning delivery while Ben finished his breakfast and cleaned up. This was all making sense. How could Ben lead his team if he didn't have a more detailed understanding of what each of them did and the processes they endure to do it?

"Okay, where were we," Chief said as he walked through the store towards Ben. "Right, technical skills. When you read comic books, this is what creates the exciting action scenes: technically proficient goliaths fighting technically proficient goliaths. Big explosions, bullets whizzing through the air, fists flying at super-speed with super-strength. It makes for a fun read. But this is rarely how our superheroes defeat their nemeses."

"What do you mean?" Ben asked. "Fighting is how most of the villains are taken down."

"From solely a skills perspective, you'd be amazed how evenly matched the superheroes and villains are. To win, superheroes must out-maneuver and out-think their adversaries." Chief paused for dramatic effect. "Just look at Tony Stark, aka Iron Man. He's considered to be one of the most intelligent characters in the comic book world."

"I can see that. In the first movie, Stark created his Iron Man suit when being held captive in a cave. It even had a new-age pacemaker that kept him from dying."

"It's actually called a 'chest repulsor transmitter,' but I'm not going to nitpick. While the Iron Man suit provides the muscle, it's Stark's conceptual skills that make him the master tactician and scientist he is."

"When you say 'conceptual skills,' you're talking about intelligence, right?" Ben asked.

"That's one aspect, but let's change the framework a bit. As nice as it may be to possess innate intellectual acumen, think of it more as intelligence learned over time."

"So true," Ben interjected. "I've known plenty of leaders who don't have the smarts of a Tony Stark, but are geniuses in their industry."

"These individuals," Chief continued, "are able to recognize how the various functions of the organization interrelate. They understand how one piece depends on another and how changing it will affect the other parts. At the same time, on a larger scale, they're able to envision how the actions of their organization associate with the political, societal, and economic landscape of their industry and community."

"Sounds daunting."

"Possibly, but if it's intelligence learned over time, all you're doing is collecting knowledge and experiences and organizing it in meaningful ways. We call these 'schemas.' The idea was developed by the famed psychologist Jean Piaget. Now, I know what you're thinking, 'Didn't the philosopher Immanuel Kant come up with the idea of schema?' He did, but it was Piaget who first used it in the manner we're discussing today."

Chief paused for a laugh; he settled for Ben's amused grin before he continued.

"Tony Stark utilized all he knew and had done to create what you so crudely call a pacemaker. This became the foundation for the Iron Man suit. But it didn't end there. Stark is open to new ideas and has never stopped trying to improve the design. Every iteration of the suit has gotten better and more complex. That's what leaders do. They draw upon complex schemas to collect and organize data. The more knowledge they've collected, the more complex the idea."

"Wait, all you just said is the more I learn, the more intelligent I'll be."

"I think I said it a bit more eloquently," replied Chief. "My point is that it's not enough just to collect the knowledge. We aren't talking about intelligence for the sake of intelligence. The success of a leader depends on your ability to solve novel, ill-defined problems. This is the practical application of intelligence. More knowledge leads to more alternatives and strategies. And those alternatives and strategies become our problem-solving skills."

"Can you go a little deeper into 'ill-defined' problems?" Ben asked. This idea resonated with him.

"As the leader, there's an expectation that you will identify and understand problems. Very often, no one is going to tell you something is wrong. In fact, my experience dictates that many avoid telling the leader the brutal realities of the situation. Some may not want to face the hard truths..."

"...or admit failures," Ben added.

"So it's up to the leader to dig. You need to know the details, the inner workings of the organization. Get out of your office and ask questions. Body language, inflections, the general flow of the team. These are key indicators of whether something is not quite right."

Ben didn't notice that he had started to grin and shake his head.

"What's so amusing?" Chief asked.

"It just occurred to me what James is doing when he's 'innocently' walking around. I always wondered how he knew everything going on with every person in every department."

"Yeah, James' casual conversations are fact-finding missions. The accumulation of what he learns on these missions pinpoints problem areas, and James, being an intelligent, well-informed leader, is prepared to deal with them. Plus, the quality of his solutions are better since he's collected all the necessary information from the sources, without relying on second-hand rumors."

Chief took care of another delivery while Ben reflected on James' investigatory skills. When Chief returned, Ben had one more nagging issue to address before he had to get to the office.

"I've already started to do some of the things we discussed and I know I need to spend more time out on the floor talking to people. What else can I do to get a jump-start on my competence?"

"How do Wonder Woman, Tony Stark, and every other superhero do it?" Chief asked.

"Tights and muscles?" Ben teased.

"They have intellectual curiosity and a drive to incessantly upgrade their skills. Truly great leadership does not happen without hard work behind it. Sure, opportunities may fall in your lap; you never know when you'll be exposed to a radioactive meteorite that will give you superpowers. But it takes a special person to seize the opportunities presented and do something constructive with them. With all of Stark's God-given intelligence, it's the effort he puts into being Iron Man that makes the difference. The suit already exists; he doesn't need to keep refining it. Besides, he's wealthy enough to not have to try as hard as he does."

"And Wonder Woman underwent years of arduous training even though she was already the queen-to-be," Ben added.

"Exactly. People like Tony Stark and Wonder Woman are never satisfied. Scholars call this Self-Determination Theory. It revolves around our intrinsic need to reach our full potential."

"I feel like I know plenty of people who aren't trying to do this."

"Possibly, but I consider this to be a universal necessity. Anyone who isn't actively striving to grow is lacking the building blocks to absolute happiness. Now I'm not saying your life isn't complete if you're not in a leadership role. You just need to be making an effort to get better at something, anything."

"So how can I improve my skills?" Ben repeated.

"When you mentioned Wonder Woman, she trained with the other people in her tribe. That's something all leaders need to do. You can't learn everything required by the job through books or by locking yourself behind a computer all day. We discussed the benefits of walking around, but it's more than just collecting information. Learning and fighting alongside her people improved Wonder Woman's skills while also legitimizing her status as royalty. She earned their respect when they saw how talented she was and how hard she practiced."

"Same thing with Aquaman," said Ben. "Nothing spoke more powerfully to the citizens of Sub Diego than when he worked side by side with them rebuilding the city. Many who were skeptical before were convinced when he backed up his words with action."

"You have been reading," Chief said. "More important than what is said is what is done. For others to rally around a leader, the leader must become a living representation of the ideals and culture of the organization. Leaders live in a fish bowl. Get it? Fish bowl? Aquaman? Come on, that was gold."

While he didn't show it, Ben had to admit it was funny.

"As Aquaman became more hands-on, he was able to hone his communication skills. For a leader, this competence cannot be downplayed. Anyway, getting back to our original point, leaders and superheroes are like everyone else – they must practice."

"I was hoping for a shortcut," Ben said.

"Sorry, dedication towards the pursuit of perfection is a long road. It requires exertion, repetition, and the occasional setback."

"Setbacks?" questioned Ben.

"You've gotta be like Resurrection Man."

"You're making that up. There's no way a superhero is named Resurrection Man."

"His name is Mitch Shelley and he was a lawyer from South Carolina before becoming an unwilling test subject for experimentation by an evil corporation. The experiments made him immortal, albeit with a twist. Whenever Shelley dies, he returns to life with a new superpower that correlates in some way to how he was last killed. If he perishes by fire, he may come back with fire-retardant skin. If he drowns, he may come back with gills."

"As envious as I am of Resurrection Man, I do not foresee a Resurrection Career."

"Mitch Shelley's lesson is to learn from your mistakes. Sure, there will be setbacks; if you don't have any, you aren't taking enough chances. Just don't dwell on what you should have done differently or sulk over what might have been. Learn from your gaffes and move on. Resurrection Man gains powers; you need to gain skills."

"What if I want to avoid mistakes?" questioned Ben.

"It's worth a shot, but you can't avoid all mistakes. However, you'll make less if you preemptively find things that will challenge you in ways you can't imagine on your own. That's why I look for an archenemy."

"Seriously? You look for an evil nemesis?"

"I didn't say anything about evil," Chief replied. "I said archenemy. You know, opponents, rivals. I seek out people who are better than me at something and will push me to up my game. You see, a while back, I was feeling a bit too high and mighty. In the course of building a successful business, I had unwittingly surrounded myself with people who inherently agree with me. Some may enjoy this feeling of supremacy, but I could feel myself becoming arrogant, out of touch."

"How did you realize this was happening?"

"This comic book store was a new venture at the time. It was my Fortress of Solitude – a side business to help me relax from 'real work.' I had made some personal connections with a few customers, but this one guy stood out. He was a real self-starter with a good mind for business. One afternoon he pitched me his latest concept, a great concept, and I ignored it for no better reason than my ego got in the way. When his plan came to fruition I jumped on board, but I've always regretted not being more open to his idea from the beginning."

"What happened to him?"

"I hired him."

"Because he was successful?"

"Because he made me think. I had the power and the money but this guy had the courage to disagree with me. He challenged me...still does, actually."

Ben thought about T. Thomas Tylerson and the Gulag Corp. That was his archenemy.

"You look like you have someone in mind," Chief said. "Tylerson's a tough bird and a worthy adversary. Many a person lacks the mental fortitude to pull a Resurrection Man..."

"Wait, how do you know about Tylerson?" Ben interrupted.

Chief did not break his stride as he continued, "...just remember, a rival doesn't have to be a person. It can be an unexpected deadline, a stumbling block, a barrier. Heck, some of my best competitors are close friends who are willing to engage in debate. The 'archenemy' is simply something that will press you to do something in a new, innovative way."

Before Ben could follow up on his question, a crowd of customers walked into the store. Chief was slammed so Ben said a quick good bye and headed to work.

The Fourth Power

THE POWER OF COMPETENCE

There is no substitute for being knowledgeable and skilled.

11

A Colorful Insignia On Your Chest Only Gets You So Far

On Ben's drive into the office, he decided to spend a chunk of the afternoon in the section of his department he was least familiar. With a mental blueprint of the office setup, he went one by one through each subdivision.

Account representatives? Check. Marketing? Check. Media relations? Check. Creative? Ugh.

Ben let out an audible groan when he realized he'd be locked in an office space with what others nicknamed the 'Doom n' Gloom Patrol.' More affectionately called the 'Artsy Annex' of the department, the creative team was made up of Cliff, Larry, and Rita. They were an odd mix of digital, graphic, and video artists. Each was a genius in his or her specialty but they had some tough personalities.

In the past, Ben's exposure to the Creative division had been limited. He would walk in with an idea and find their draft on his desk the next day. If he liked the draft, he'd follow up with a thank you. If he had changes, he'd brace himself for the inevitable backlash. As much as they fought with each other, when one of them was under attack, which could involve no more than a minor critique of a work product, they would unite against their common foe with an endless wave of hipster sarcasm and judgmental comments. Ben had been on the receiving end multiple times.

When Ben approached the Artsy Annex, he came bearing cookies. It was a cheap ploy, but if it reduced just a little tension, it was worth it.

Cliff, Larry, and Rita were throwing their usual jibes at each other until Ben walked in. Ben explained he was interested in learning more about what they do. He apologized for not doing this sooner and, in a desperate attempt to lighten the mood, offered them the treats.

Ben sensed their skepticism as they reluctantly took a cookie. He made an effort to be self-deprecating, but that did not get a reaction. He asked a harmless question about the high-tech printer, but the response was guarded. Then, without putting too much thought into it, Ben said, "Cliff, with all those computer pieces spread out on your desk, your work station has a very Oracle-like look about it."

"Excuse me?" Cliff asked.

"You know, Oracle. Barbara Gordon? The original Batgirl?"

The minute Ben said this he could feel the vibe change. His off-the-cuff pop-culture reference resonated with the team. They were instantly more receptive. It turned out all three were huge comic book fans.

The remaining hours were surprisingly enjoyable. Cliff, Larry, and Rita were not nearly as 'Doom n' Gloom' as Ben had expected. Their interactions were amusing as they took turns having fun at each other's expense.

Ben spent time with each of them to get an overview of how they performed their jobs and engaged them as a group to understand how work flowed through their division. He was not naïve enough to think he fully comprehended the complexity of their responsibilities, but he knew more than when he started.

"Maybe I've misread them," Ben thought. "Maybe their seemingly malicious comments were attempts at humor."

It was at this moment Mary Jane came in with edits. The fun evaporated from the room and was replaced with a dark cloud. Mary Jane was polite, but she was noticeably rushing through her revisions so she could get out as quickly as possible.

"What was that?" Ben asked after Mary Jane left.

"What was what?" Larry replied.

"That attitude. Did Mary Jane do something to offend you? What's the problem?"

Like trying to drink from a fire hose, Cliff, Larry, and Rita all started talking at once about how the Creative division was treated like second-class members of the department. At first it sounded petty, but the more they spoke and the more examples they provided, it became clear there were legitimate concerns. Too often, ideas were generated without their input and dumped in their inbox.

"Is that what you were so angry about a few days ago?" Ben asked. He thought about when he had been rushing to the

Gulag meeting. Ben heard them arguing but he was in such a frenzied state at the time that he didn't address it.

"I think the frustration built up that morning," said Cliff. "We worked on the visuals for the Gulag pitch for weeks. When the time came to present and hear the client's feedback, every division of this department was represented except ours."

"Even before that, we weren't included in any of the brainstorming sessions leading up to the final proposal," Rita interjected.

"I'll tell you what – I will get you a seat at the table. You'll be more involved at the front-end and have greater exposure to clients."

"But...?" Rita hesitantly said.

"But you need to meet me halfway."

"How so?" asked Cliff.

"The first step will involve being more approachable. Participation means being open to differing ideas without making snide comments or smug facial expressions. I want to see the upbeat social skills of Spider-Man, not the brooding grouchiness of Hancock."

"Hancock?" Larry laughed. "You did not just use a Will Smith reference."

"I did. It was a good movie and I stand by it," teased Ben. "So do we have a deal?"

Ben received emphatic agreement as he walked out of Creative with an empty cookie plate and a renewed sense of confidence.

12

The Power of Collaboration

Ben left work feeling like he was on top of the world. He still wasn't thrilled with the lack of progress on the Gulag pitch, but after facing (and considering himself victorious against) the Creative division, it felt good to have a win.

Not yet ready to call it a day, Ben decided to stop in the comic book shop again. No agenda, no meeting with Chief; Ben just wanted to peruse the shelves and maybe find something interesting. He could justify it as research, but who was he kidding? Ben was enjoying the comic book world.

"You look happy," Chief said when he saw Ben sifting through a bin of older comics.

Ben relayed his adventure in the Artsy Annex. He made sure to emphasize the Power of Competence so Chief would know he was remaining true to the Pledge.

"Bravo! It sounds like you discovered the cumulative strength of the Powers," Chief said after Ben finished his harrowing tale.

"What do you mean?"

"An environmentally-conscious superhero once said, 'By your powers combined, I am Captain Planet.' Well, with these Leadership Powers combined, you are an effective leader. You see, the Powers all work together. More competence made you more persuasive. As you said, 'the Creatives' are a difficult group. They listened because you knew what you were talking about. Making an impact boosted your self-confidence, which fed into your feeling of accountability to address their issues. Then, with a solid grasp on the subject matter and a connection with the team, you were able to form a more persuasive argument and move the group towards your vision. In one sitting you've applied all of the Powers."

"Wait, didn't you say there were five Powers? Competence, Persuasive, Accountability, Conviction – that's only four."

"Are we trying to make you a better leader or accountant?" joked Chief. "You touched on the fifth without even knowing it."

Before Ben could get an explanation, a few people gathered near a display in the middle of the store. "What a night to show up," Chief said to Ben. "My Council gathers once a month. Great group, you'll love 'em."

In an exaggerated, old-time circus ringleader intonation Chief announced, "Gathered together from the cosmic reaches of the universe – here in this great hall of justice – are the most powerful forces of good ever assembled."

Thankfully, Olsen, who seemed to be a member of this prestigious group, whispered that the speech was from the opening of the old *Super Friends* cartoon. It's how Chief started every Council meeting.

For the next hour, Chief facilitated one of the most captivating discussions Ben had ever witnessed. He only knew a third of the comic book characters mentioned and was oblivious to many of the current event references and business theories, but the debates were fascinating. Ben had never seen anyone challenge Chief. Chief gave as good as he took, but he was chastened more than once.

The meeting broke up as fast as it started.

"What was that?" Ben still could not wrap his head around it.

"That's my Council. My brain trust. My 'League of Extraordinary Gentleman.'"

"That's not what I mean. You seemed to have total control without any indication of authority."

"I don't have any authority. They participated because they want to."

"Incredible."

"Is it?" Chief questioned. "Do you think it takes power to get someone to listen? You may have a fancy job title, but don't kid yourself. Any member of your team can disregard you and your directives whenever they so choose. Will there be consequences? Sure, but they have free will and the ability to ignore you."

"Then how did you do it? What was the technique?"

"Do you know what they call a leader without followers?" Chief smirked. "Lonely."

Chief waited a beat for Ben to laugh. When it didn't happen, he continued.

"There are hundreds of definitions for a leader, but the only one that matters is a leader is someone who others want to follow. You can't do it all yourself, and why would you want to? My best ideas happen when I'm bouncing them off other people. Anyway, where's the fun in celebrating a win or commiserating a loss in an empty room? So when you asked about my technique, what we're talking about is the way I build relationships. It's also our fifth Leadership Power and something you've been inadvertently doing all week – the Power of Collaboration:

The key to achieving a goal is to involve others.

"This is where the leader actually leads. Anyone can direct people to do their bidding; it takes a true leader to collaborate."

"I'm not sure I understand the distinction," Ben said.

"Dictators dictate orders. People then follow these orders and things get done. Effective today, not so much in the future. Leaders, true leaders, use all the Powers we've discussed to build connections with others. Relationships, man. Not superficial, insincere banter but a meaningful use of social intelligence to understand why the people around you do what they do."

Ben gave a quizzical look before Chief continued.

"This may sound overly complicated, but all I'm saying is you need to treat people like people. Don't view your team as disposable objects that can be easily replaced. If this is how you feel, either replace them or yourself. Either way, there's no need to be a jerk."

"I don't think I've been a jerk," Ben thought.

"I don't think you've been a jerk, Ben..."

"How does he read my mind?" Ben thought.

"...but if you want to build a solid work group with self-sustaining, high-performance goals, focus your attention on the human aspects of your teammates. What gets them excited? What type of atmosphere can you construct that will build trust? Are you flexible enough to blend others' ideas into your own or, even more, open enough to choose their ideas over yours? How do you demonstrate that you value their viewpoints and ideas? These are the cornerstones of collaboration."

"So that is what your Council provides?" Ben asked. "They are the group you've assembled to help you work through problems? Like a personal advisory board?"

"When we discussed the Power of Competence, I mentioned the need to find a nemesis, someone who can challenge you. For the Power of Collaboration, find people who support you. Not necessarily folks who agree with you per se, but those who want to see you and your vision succeed."

"Can these be one in the same?" asked Ben.

"Sure, just look at the Thing."

"You mean the big, orange rock-covered guy?"

"That's the one. On the Collaboration side, he enjoys 'clobberin'' the bad guys alongside the other members of the Fantastic Four. He admires their heroism and enjoys their fellowship. On the Competence side, the Thing recognizes that while the rest of the team is inferior to him in raw power, they excel in ways he does not. He sees this as an opportunity to learn and grow from his peers."

"So you want peers in your support system," Ben confirmed.

"You bet. No one is successful on their own; leaders must forge strong alliances with others. Surround yourself with internal allies. They might be friends, they might be co-workers, they might be both. As powerful as the Thing is alone, the Fantastic Four together are unstoppable."

"What about the people who report to me? Would you consider them internal allies?" Ben asked.

"In a way, but, by definition, you are not on equal footing. In superhero terms, let's call them sidekicks."

"This seems like a demeaning term," Ben noted.

"It can be, depending on how it's used. The disparaging use of 'sidekicks' is associated with the villains. Harley Quinn is considered to be Joker's sidekick. In reality, she's more of a lackey. Otis, who we discussed earlier, was the same thing for Lex. They do what they're told and are treated poorly in the process. They are intended to remain underlings. The only way Harley, Otis, or any of the other villainous sidekicks will move up in the ranks is to take out their boss."

"The bad guys do tend to lack loyalty," Ben added.

"Conversely, the hero's sidekick is a superhero in the making. This is someone who, if successful, will one day be on their own and serve alongside the hero as an equal. Most of the greats have a sidekick. Green Arrow has spent considerable time training and teaching Speedy, just as Captain America has Bucky, Big Daddy has Hit Girl, the Tick has Arthur, and Batman has his cave full of sidekicks.

"I've always considered Batman to be more of a loner," Ben said.

"He might enjoy this reputation, but Batman has more sidekicks than anyone. He's surrounded by capable people who can take care of themselves, each other, and him. They share the same goal to keep Gotham City safe and propagate Batman's vision when he isn't around. Batman figured out a long time ago that the key to achieving a goal is to involve others. Just look at Dick Grayson. Dick was the original Robin before he branched out on his own to become Nightwing. Dick was then 'promoted' to become Batman when Bruce Wayne was out of commission. And he was great. You know why? Because Bruce is a master collaborator."

"A master collaborator?"

Chief called Olsen back over to the discussion.

"Quick exercise. Olsen, come here for a sec. I liked that game at the diner. Let's do a lightning round. Ben, you name a characteristic of a person who excels at collaboration; Olsen, you give me a superhero. On your mark, get set--"

"Compassionate," Ben blurted out.

"Explain," Chief pressed.

"Ultimately, it's about treating people with respect. Leaders need to be empathetic, supportive, and show concern for others. Displaying sensitivity and altruism wouldn't hurt either."

"Olsen?"

"I know it's generic, but Superman is one of the more compassionate superheroes."

"I'll decide if it's generic," Chief winked. "Go on."

"*Superman #701*, the "Grounded" storyline. This is the one where Superman walks across America to rediscover truth, justice, and the American way. Along his travels, he helps a man fix his car, uses his x-ray vision to diagnose a man with heart problems, and burns down a drug dealer's house."

"Nice examples, but where's the compassion?" Ben quipped.

"It's in Superman's final endeavor. There's a woman on the ledge of a building who is thinking about jumping. She feels hopeless, like her life is meaningless. Faced with this obstacle, Superman has a few options. The easy answer is to fly up and bring her safely to the ground. She'd be out of harm's way for the time being, but this would not alleviate the problem. His second course of action would be to walk by and let her do what she's going to do."

"That does not seem in character with Superman," Ben remarked.

"It's not. I'm just going through the possibilities," Olsen said defensively. "Finally, what Superman actually did was stop and talk to her. He listened to her problems and made an effort to show her that life may be worth living."

Chief jumped in. "I think Superman said something like, 'All I know is we have to try. That's what life is. We try. We push back, against the darkness, just a little.' Nice example, Olsen. Very touching. Ben, numero dos."

"Approachability."

"Easy to say," Chief scowled, "but if I hear one more manager tell me they have an open-door policy, I'm going to attack 'em. Great, your door's open. Now how can you actually be more approachable?"

"This was a good question," thought Ben. He had just discussed the need to be more approachable with the Creatives but he didn't articulate it quite as well as he would have liked.

"They can be humble," Olsen interrupted.

"Good answer, Olsen. For this one, you describe and Ben's going to give the superhero."

"Okay, humbleness is about exhibiting humility. They see their role not in terms of self-aggrandizement but as a means to serve the greater good. It's the same thing that distinguishes the hero from the villain – the hero is trying to save people while the villain wants attention and credit."

"Nicely done," Chief nodded. "Ben?"

Ben stammered. This was not in his wheelhouse, but he'd give it a shot. "I'm not sure which movie it was, but there was this one Viking superhero who ended up joining the superhero team the Avengers with the Hulk and Iron Man."

"You mean Thor?" Olsen laughed. "The God of Thunder?"

"That's the one. Thor was a heroic and brave crown prince with a strong track record of leading his people into battle. Unfortunately, he was also arrogant and headstrong. In the first movie, his egotistical actions led to a broken truce with some ice monsters."

"Frost Giants of Jotunheim," spurted Chief and Olsen like contestants on a game show.

"Anyway," continued Ben, "seeing as Thor nearly started a superfluous war, his father, the mighty king, realized Thor was not yet ready to succeed him on the throne. To build character and teach some humility, Thor was exiled to Earth where he was stripped of his powers and his weapons. With time, Thor learned to care more about protecting the innocent than the savagery of war. He still enjoyed a good fight, but was now more self-effacing."

"I totally agree," said Chief. "The only thing I'd like to add is that approachability needs vulnerability. If the leader seems too perfect, no one will freely admit slipups."

"I've never heard of being perfect as a problem," Ben said.

"That's because we're all trying so hard to be seen as faultless. Now I'm not saying the leader should be error-prone, just that it's okay to admit blunders and be a bit self-deprecating. Inject a little humor; divulge embarrassing stories to show you're human. Remember when we were discussing relatability as a means to influence others? Well, it's also effective in teamwork. It allows others to feel a connection beyond boss/subordinate."

"Do superheroes really do this?" Ben asked.

"Are you kidding," answered Olsen. "Spider-Man is always cracking jokes. So are Flash, Deadpool, Nightwing, Plastic Man, and many more. It diffuses potentially tense situations, builds rapport, and provides some necessary levity. I remember this one time, Spider-Man says to Grey Goblin--"

"Harrumph!" Chief exaggeratedly cleared his throat. "Getting back to the characteristics of master collaborators, so far we have compassion and humbleness. Give me one more, Ben."

"I'd like to go back to the concept of sidekicks. Collaboration requires a willingness to teach others what you know. Great leaders should be great coaches."

"Sounds hokey," grumbled Olsen.

"He's right, Olsen," said Chief. According to Hersey-Blanchard's leadership model, the most important factor affecting a leader's effectiveness is their ability to develop their staff. Leaders need to take a personal interest in guiding and educating others so as to help broaden thinking, share experiences, and pinpoint each individual's specific talents and willingness to take on additional responsibilities."

"Okay, but does this take a lot of extra time?" Olsen questioned.

"It shouldn't," Ben said. It felt good to finally be able to support Chief. "Developing others is part of a supervisor's job. If leaders can maintain the mindset that they are teachers, they'll have a more capable and motivated staff. Once this culture is in place, it should free up the leader to do other things."

"I've seen studies showing a 25-40 percent increase in productivity when the boss serves as a mentor," added Chief.

"I stand corrected," said Olsen. "Let's see if I can make up for my ignorance with an example."

"What do you think, Ben," Chief nodded. "Do we have this one covered?"

The Fifth Power

THE POWER OF COLLABORATION

The key to achieving a goal is to involve others.

13

Who Leads The Leader?

The next day did not go quite as well as Ben had hoped. In fact, it was downright abysmal. The big ideas for the Gulag campaign hadn't panned out. Every concept mentioned was either too monotonous, too cliché, or too forgettable.

How could it be so difficult to sell a sports drink?

On the plus side, the team was collaborating better then Ben had ever seen – the Creatives were making constructive contributions, everyone was participating, and the pressure had not yet led to a single blow-up. They were close once when Rita and Mary Jane disagreed on a tagline, but Ben took charge and facilitated a peaceful resolution.

What a difference a week had made. Before learning the Powers, Ben was sure he would not have addressed Rita and Mary Jane's dispute. He would have remained focused on the task at hand and hoped the quarrel would resolve itself.

It took some pressure off knowing everyone was working well together, but this did not change the fact that T. Thomas

Tylerson was going to be here in less than thirty-six hours and they had nothing.

Ben's team had broken for dinner so he had a sliver of time to mope before reconvening. Just as he sat down and closed his eyes, James knocked and walked into Ben's office.

"My sources tell me you and your team and settling in for a long night. How're you holding up?"

"I've had worse days, but not many. I thought we'd turned a corner, but instead we hit another wall."

"It's frustrating to be so close before losing it. Sometimes it's easier to start from scratch," James reassured Ben.

"That's the plan. Just trying to figure out the best way to broach this with the others."

"I know you have Chief's advice in your head so I won't pile on."

"Except to say what?" Ben knew something was on James' mind. The more he learned, the more he realized James did not have idle conversations.

"Chief is teaching you well," James smiled. "I was just going to stress the need for collaboration. You have an entire team that appears to be dedicated to helping you be successful. May I add how impressive that is? I've never seen someone implement Chief's playbook with such immediate results."

"Thanks, but right now I think I need his Council more than his playbook."

"Yeah, it's a good group."

"Do you have a Council like Chief's?"

"Mine's not quite as formal, but yes, I have a council of sorts. I'd call it a collection of alliances."

"So how do you build these alliances?" asked Ben.

"I start by remaining open to new opportunities. Let me tell you about one of my partnerships. When I first got started in marketing, I had an account with this dinky diner."

"The diner you own?"

"I'm only a part-owner, but yes, same place. I met with the owner and hung around for a few days to observe the operations. The problem wasn't how the place was managed and it certainly wasn't the food. The issue was with the lack of publicity. Nobody had heard of it. My background in marketing and passion for the product could help, but the owner had mounting debt and couldn't afford to pay me. So we created a win/win. I agreed to trade my expertise and time for a small stake in the ownership. It was a gamble."

"If it was the same diner you introduced to me, you made a wise bet."

"I was lucky."

"How can you say that?" Ben questioned.

"You can attribute success to hard work and know-how, but the simple truth is I've been fortunate to garner more wins then losses."

"Calling it luck understates your accomplishments," Ben said, not sure why he felt the need to defend James against himself.

"Maybe luck is not an accurate term. Remaining open to my surroundings has led me towards lucky outcomes. I've met the right people at the right time. That partnership with the diner came about because I was hanging out in this comic book shop. I was chatting with one of the guys when he mentioned having the best French toast of his life at this little place that was on its last leg. I sampled it the next morning.

And then the next. It became my personal mission to save that restaurant; everyone had to know how good it was."

"And that guy in the comic book store was Chief, I'm assuming."

"Did he tell you I tried to get him involved at the beginning of the project?"

"He said his hubris got in the way," Ben declared. "That he wasn't open to the ideas of those around him."

"Chief still kicks himself for hesitating. Anyway, he was so impressed with my work on the diner that he offered me a job at his marketing firm."

"Chief owned a marketing firm?" Ben asked.

"Are you kidding?" James bellowed. "Please tell me you're kidding. You aren't kidding, are you? What do you think the 'W' stands for in POW! PR? It's 'White,' Chief's last name. He's a founding partner."

Ben almost fell over. He had no clue that he'd been hanging out with his boss's boss's boss. This explained how Chief knew so much about the business and about the Gulag account.

It took a minute for Ben to muster the words to speak. "Chief has a secret identity?"

"Apparently, it was only a secret to you."

"So why have I never seen him around?"

"Chief gave up his office a long time ago for Blaze Comics. He runs POW! PR, a news magazine conglomerate, and countless other enterprises from those hallowed, comic book-filled halls."

"He runs a news magazine, too? Let me guess, he's the one who gave Olsen's work to the editor."

"That's right, detective. Chief is also responsible for speaking with Tylerson about giving your team a chance...and a second chance."

"How'd he know about me?" Ben asked.

"Chief is aware of every campaign we pitch."

"Power of Competence?"

"Power of Competence. Chief knows the details of POW! PR even if he's not physically here to observe them. He relies on people like me to introduce him to up-and-coming talent."

"You really are a superhero, James. If I haven't thanked you before, let me just say I am proud to be your sidekick."

"It is my pleasure. I'm calling it a night, Ben. Give me a ring if there's anything I can do to help."

"Thanks, James. Not just for your offer, but for everything."

"That's what superheroes are for, boy wonder," James said with a wink.

A few minutes later, Mary Jane came in with a familiar-looking styrofoam container.

"Thought you might be hungry," Mary Jane said. "The team's all over the place but they asked me to thank you for ordering real food for dinner. They were expecting lukewarm pizza, so a meal from that fancy diner up the street was an unanticipated treat."

"It's a new favorite place of mine. Anyway, I hope it shows how much I appreciate all of your hard work. It's been a long week and everyone's given more than 100 percent."

"Can I ask you something?" Mary Jane asked.

"Of course," Ben said, moving his food to the side of the desk.

"What happened to you this week?"

"How do you mean?"

"You seem different. It's hard for me to put my finger on it, but it's as if you have more control while simultaneously being less controlling. It's like a Bizzaro version of Ben."

Ben chuckled to himself as he thought about the Bizzaro character from the comic books – a supervillain who was a mirror image of Superman, but opposite and rather demented. Ben hoped his previous leadership style was Bizzaro Ben and this new and improved version was the real deal.

"Yeah, it's been quite a week," Ben responded.

"About that," Mary Jane said, "I've been thinking about our conversation a few nights ago. You asked me to give you a chance before deciding whether to transfer to a different department."

"Here it comes," thought James. He braced himself for the worst.

"I've made my decision," Mary Jane continued. "Through a lot of soul-searching and thinking about my future at POW! PR, if it's all right with you, regardless of what happens with Tylerson, I'd like to stay with this team."

Ben almost fell out of his chair with surprise.

"Are you kidding? Of course!" Ben got up and gave her a hug, just another example of something he would have never done pre-Chief.

"What did it?" asked Ben.

"You. I was on the fence, but the way you've been leading the team this week has been uplifting. In the midst of impending doom, you've not only held us together, but strengthened us as a team. I made my final decision in today's meeting."

"What happened in the meeting?"

"When Rita and I went off the handle a bit, you calmed us both down and guided us towards conciliation."

Ben was stunned and a little confused.

"There was a compromise, Mary Jane, but in all fairness, didn't Rita end up coming out ahead?"

"I don't need a leader who lets me do whatever I want, Ben. I want someone who's fair and not afraid to make the tough choices. With Rita and me, you didn't jump to conclusions; you listened to both sides and made a rational assessment based on the facts. It didn't even matter that you like me more," Mary Jane teased. "I respect your stand and the upbeat manner in which you did it. This type of leadership is what's convinced me to bet my career on you and this team."

"No pressure there," half-joked Ben.

"Damn right there's pressure. We have a day and a half before Tylerson's here and I want to win. What we need is to tell a story, a really super story."

"Sorry, what did you just say?"

"We need a super story. You know, something that'll impress Tylerson."

Ben sprung out of his chair with excitement. "Get the team together and tell them to meet me at this location in a half hour."

Ben scribbled an address on a piece of paper, handed it to Mary Jane, and ran out the door.

When the team pulled up to Blaze Comics, Ben was standing in front of the store with Olsen.

"Everyone, I'd like to introduce you to Olsen, our new freelance storyteller. He has some ideas that are really super."

14

The Superpowered Leader

On this cool spring morning, Virginia walked into work with eager apprehension. She'd been at POW! PR for nearly three years, but today was different. Today was her first day as a supervisor.

When she exited the elevator onto the floor housing her new department, Virginia looked to her left where she paid special attention to the wall of awards and trophies, most dated in the last year or so. On her right hung framed samples of past advertising campaigns. With the achievements so prominently displayed, there was no way to avoid the looming pressures of working with such an accomplished team.

"You can do this," Virginia unconvincingly assured herself. "It's too late to get nervous; this is why you're here!"

Virginia had graduated at the top of her class before accepting an entry-level position with POW! PR. She had her pick of all the top PR firms but chose this one due to its reputation for what multiple professors had declared the most innovative marketing in the last decade. Never before had a line of sports drinks been promoted in such a manner. Some praised the story this campaign was telling, while others just thought it looked "very cool." Either way, POW! PR's work had propelled Gulag from a small, regionally known drink to an international brand in record time.

Since joining POW! PR, Virginia had paid her dues. She'd done some impressive work and gotten the attention of the top leaders. Now she was joining the Incredibles, a team considered to be not just the gold standard of POW! PR, but the gold standard of the marketing industry.

Her new supervisor position was created as a result of the department's rapid expansion. She'd gone through an arduous selection process to receive this coveted position with the most coveted of teams. Now it was time to earn it.

When Virginia arrived in the work area of the department, it was abuzz with activity. Before she could get lost in the chaos, a woman yelled, "Ben, she's here!"

"Thanks, Betty. Ms. Potts, we are so excited you're joining our team," Ben declared as he walked towards Virginia with his hand extended.

Lowering his voice, Ben continued without pausing, "Why don't you throw your stuff in my office. We have a big meeting and this'll be a great chance to see us tick."

Ben then ushered Virginia down the hall to a large conference hall. There was already a large gathering of people but Ben found her a comfortable seat near the front.

"All right, all right, everyone settle down. Good morning, good morning. We have a lot to cover. Let me start by introducing you to Virginia. Today's her first day with us, so please make her feel welcome and don't scare her off."

Virginia recognized most of the people in the room but hadn't formally met any of them. That would happen later. For now, she was happy to blend in and observe.

"Olsen, you're up," Ben said.

"Thanks, B. I was speaking with some people at Gulag last week and they mentioned incorporating a few other lines of business into our superhero-themed sports drink promotion. I think I have the story, but I'd like to bounce it off all of you before we continue. What I have is good, but I need something transcending."

After hearing Olsen's pitch, the room erupted with questions and ideas. Once it settled down, Olsen looked at Virginia.

"You've been quiet. What are your thoughts?" He then stared at Virginia for what felt like hours.

"I think it's, um, nice," Virginia said. How could she question the great Olsen? He was a legend at POW! PR.

"Nice? That's what I say when Rita tries to bake banana bran muffins. No offense, Rita," Olsen said half-jokingly.

"None taken," Rita responded as she playfully threw a crumpled piece of paper at him.

"Give me some feedback, Virginia. There's a reason people call this team the Incredibles and not the Uncredibles. We collaborate, even if we're disagreeing."

"Okay," Virginia said hesitantly. "Can I start by saying I haven't even been working here for an hour?"

"You may not. Please continue," Olsen said.

Virginia started with some light edits, but as she became more comfortable, her critiques became sharper. By the time she finished, Olsen had a notepad full of ideas.

Per Ben's instructions, Virginia spent the rest of the day with everyone in the department. She expected the high level of professionalism, but was amazed at how much fun everyone seemed to be having. She had been told this team was different, and she could feel it.

The Incredibles were immediately trusting and willing to share whatever they knew without barriers or trepidation. Virginia had expected some degree of reverence seeing how she was now in management, but they didn't seem concerned. Everyone was treated with the same level of friendliness and respect.

As the day wrapped up, Ben walked into her office and sat down.

"So, how was your first day?"

Virginia started to go through a timeline of the day. Ben stopped her before she had a chance to explain the entire itinerary.

"Let me rephrase. I know what you did today. I'm more interested in your impressions of the department."

"It was good. I think it was good," Virginia stammered.

Sensing her uneasiness, Ben jumped in.

"Really? My first day, heck, my first six months as a supervisor were terrifying. I didn't know how I was supposed to act or what I was supposed to do. I was thrown in with a bunch of people who were great at their jobs and didn't seem to need any leadership. I can't tell you how many times I sat in my car dreading having to walk into this place."

"Seriously? You look like you have it all together. I can't imagine you being scared. Do you know people in other departments call you Mr. Incredible?"

"I'm flattered, but Mr. Incredible has a much better physique. Anyway, I don't look good in red spandex."

"I guess I'm not sure why I'm here."

Virginia immediately regretted saying this. Why did she feel comfortable speaking so frankly to Ben? They barely knew each other.

"Don't get me wrong," Virginia backpedaled, "I really want this job and to be a part of this team."

"First, take a deep breath. If we're going to work together, you need to know it's okay to tell me how you feel. Being a leader can be a lonely job."

"How do you deal with the loneliness?" she asked.

"I used to hold it in and pretend like everything was fine. Then a wise man taught me that there are more productive ways to react. Now, I have a League."

"A League?"

"Some call it a council, others a collection of alliances. Mine's a League. Regardless of the name, what's important is having a group of people you can rely on for honest feedback...but let's not jump ahead. For now, I just want you to focus on feeling accountable for your new position. You earned it," Ben assured her. "Do you know why we chose you for this job? Out of the hundreds of applicants, why it was you?"

This had been eating away at Virginia for weeks, but every time she thought about what made her so special, the burden of having to prove it was overwhelming.

"It was your marketing campaign for the diner down the street."

Virginia remembered that pitch well. It was one of the few times James, the vice president from upstairs, had attended one of her client meetings. Who would have guessed he'd be interested in a little diner?

"Do you recall near the end of your pitch when the diner owner asked you about the statistics on the franchising potential of the restaurant?"

"I think I asked one of my colleagues for the numbers?" Virginia said.

"You did more than that. In one of the first solo pitches of your career, you shared credit with someone else. You also gave kudos to the graphic artist who rendered the visuals and your Executive Director for her input."

"I needed to recognize Mary Jane. Without her, I never would have had the opportunity to handle the pitch in the first place."

Ben thought back to when he was so worried about losing Mary Jane. She was true to her word – Mary Jane never asked to leave Ben's team. But when a new Executive Director position opened up, Ben pushed and prodded her to go for it. In the short-term, it was a loss for his team; however, what type of leader would Ben be if he held someone back from reaching their potential. Mary Jane was ready and had since proven it time and again in her new role. The sidekick became the superhero and Ben had a new member of his League.

"Virginia, it was already clear you knew your subject matter, so when you shared credit in that meeting, you showed courage."

Judging by the look on her face, Ben could tell she didn't know what he meant.

"It's the type of courage that comes with not having to be the end-all, be-all. You exhibited humbleness and an ability to collaborate with others. That is what I need from the leaders on my team. When I was asking around about you, it was these people who gave you the biggest endorsements. Your style fostered their loyalty and respect. Mary Jane, your loudest supporter, would have fought to keep you except, lucky for me, she didn't have a supervisor opening."

Virginia did not know what to say. She had no idea any of this had made an impact.

"Although," Ben playfully said, "I will say that as good as your diner pitch was, their French toast sells itself."

"Thanks, Ben. I'm feeling a little better. If you don't mind me asking, how did you learn all of this?"

"Do you read comic books...?"

The Five Superpowers of Leaders

THE POWER OF ACCOUNTABILITY

Your success is rooted in how committed you are to being accountable for the outcome.

THE POWER OF CONVICTION

Your value is determined by the goals you strive for and the manner in which you achieve them.

THE POWER OF PERSUASION

Your effectiveness is based on your ability to influence others.

THE POWER OF COMPETENCE

There is no substitute for being knowledgeable and skilled.

THE POWER OF COLLABORATION

The key to achieving a goal is to involve others.

Acknowledgments

Have you ever sat through a leadership development session wondering, "How can I escape" and, with no inconspicuous getaway route, "How can I stay awake?" This was me, except I was the yawn-inspiring speaker and I was boring myself. So in the middle of one particular presentation, I deviated from my pre-planned agenda and asked –

"What makes Batman qualified to lead a group of people?"

After enduring the uncomfortable silence, one of the high-level executives in the back of the room hollered, "Finally, some useful information." His comment lessened tension, giving the room permission to engage in a serious superhero-themed conversation. A lively discussion followed where we dissected the Dark Knight's leadership style and how it can enrich our managerial role.

I could not identify who my outspoken supporter was in that session, but his reinforcement formed the impetus of *Cape, Spandex, Briefcase.*

It is not possible to list all the people who helped me find a voice through this book. Your support has and continues to be beyond measure. My utmost appreciation goes out:

To all my friends and colleagues who read the manuscript throughout the process and offered valuable insights and suggestions.

To my incredible team of editors who helped shape the inside of this manuscript to more legibly reflect my thoughts:

Robin Schroffel and the dynamic duo of Olivia Kahn and Madeline Kahn. You and the talented visual artists who made the outside of this manuscript reflect my intentions for the inside – Shelby Jones and Oz Guetta – exemplify the Power of Collaboration.

To Josh Levine who has been forcing the Power of Accountability onto me since we were kids. Glad he's in my corner.

To collect the lessons presented in this book, I have been fortunate to learn about leadership firsthand from some of the finest leaders in the business: Christopher Adams, Aaron Appleton, Dale Clift, Rosemary DuRocher, Bobby Harris, Tracy Harrison, Mary Kay Prout, Richard Rendina, Joe Steier, and Jo Ellen Unger. The ways they've lived the Power of Persuasion have heavily influenced how I understand, impart, and demonstrate leadership.

To the colleagues and sages who have influenced my thinking and may see their pearls of wisdom sprinkled throughout this book: Warren Bennis, Bob Burg, Cathy Bush, Ram Charan, Jim Collins, Kimberly Collins, Stephen Dubner, Adam Duritz, Paul Gamm, Malcolm Gladwell, Betty Hubschman, Steve King, Jonathan Leibowitz, Steven Levitt, Carmen McCrink, Sean McMahon, John Mann, Tom Morris, Kim Morrow, Burt Nanus, Donald Phillips, and Ed Russo. They are all models for the Power of Competence.

To my parents who instilled in me the Power of Conviction since before I knew it was a power. Their lifetime of unwavering support has and continues to be a source of motivation, passion, and growth. And to my sister and her family for believing I'm smarter than I really am. Their confidence inspires me to try to live up to their impressions.

To my kids for always making me smile and reminding me of what is important.

To my wife, Allison. This book would not be possible without her encouragement. She has listened to more rants about superheroes than any non-comic book reader should have to endure. I am lucky to be loved by someone who is so much cooler than me.

And finally, to all of you who read this book. Please choose to use your powers for good.

To continue on your trek towards enhanced leadership powers, David Kahn writes about leadership, success, and organizational culture at leadersayswhat.com.

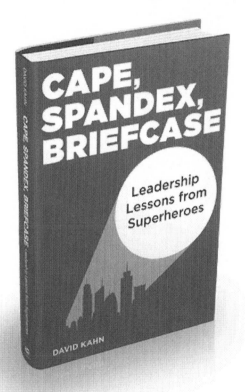

Starewell offers special discounted pricing on this title for bulk sales. Your business, nonprofit, school, house of worship, etc. can receive special discounted pricing, direct shipping, and more. Go to starewellpublishing.com for more information.

Made in the USA
Middletown, DE
05 March 2017